Dublin

Footprint

Seán Sheehan & Pat Levy

Contents

4 About the author
4 Acknowledgements

5 Introducing Dublin
6 Introduction
8 At a glance
12 Trip planner
16 Contemporary Dublin

19 Travel essentials
21 Getting there
25 Getting around
28 Tours
30 Tourist information

Guide

31 Dublin
33 Grafton Street and around
46 Temple Bar and around
53 The Liberties and west
58 Ballsbridge and south
62 O'Connell Street and around
76 From Smithfield to the Phoenix Park
82 Glasnevin and Clontarf
86 Museums and galleries

89 Around Dublin
91 South of Dublin
95 North of Dublin

Listings

103 Sleeping
125 Eating and drinking
147 Bars and clubs
159 Arts and entertainment
   161 Cinema
   164 Dance
   165 Music
   169 Theatre
173 Festivals and events
179 Shopping
191 Sports
197 Gay and lesbian
203 Kids
209 Directory

219 Background
   220 A sprint through history
   227 Art and architecture
   230 Books
   234 Language

236 Index
241 Publishing stuff
246 Advertising

247 Maps (see inside back cover for DART map)
   247 Map 1   252 Map 5
   248 Map 2   254 Map 6
   250 Map 3   256 Map 7
   251 Map 4

About the authors

Seán Sheehan was brought up in London but spent every summer holiday in Ireland. After adult years of travelling and living in southeast Asia, Seán now has his home in the west of Ireland.

Pat Levy visited West Cork one Easter when she was 19 and the memory of the spring flowers and heather on the hills has continued to draw her back like a narcotic. Author of *Culture Shock! Ireland* and co-author of a walking guide to the island, Pat is now hooked for life and she looks forward to the time when she can tend to her garden in the west of Ireland full time.

Acknowledgements

Seán Sheehan and Pat Levy would like to thank John Lahiffe at Tourism Ireland Ltd for the help and consideration he has given to the Footprint Pocket Guide to Dublin. Special thanks to everyone at Footprint who have worked so hard to get this edition out on time. Thanks also to the many patient people at Dublin Tourism who dealt with our many queries and to the people at Outhouse Gay Community and Resource Centre for their assistance.

From struggling provincial backwater to the city that never sleeps, Dublin has been riding one hell of a roller coaster for the last decade. Through the traumatic changes of recent years, Ireland's capital has regained a European presence that it last experienced towards the end of the 18th century. Every day, while Dubliners nonchalantly go about their own business, planeloads of visitors arrive in this city to party. Temple Bar ladles on the blarney as thick as the head on a glass of Guinness, while wood-panelled Edwardian pubs and trad musicians in Aran sweaters jostle for position with beech and steel café-bars, hip nightclubs, chic shops and high-tech arts centres.

Yet, amid the sophisticated gloss, the fiddly-diddly music and the political wheeler-dealing is a city whose secrets are still waiting to be explored. Dublin is skirted to the south by the brown-green slopes of the Wicklow Mountains and the great curve of Dublin Bay, and through the heart of it all snakes the Liffey: dark, unfathomable and just a little bit muddier than we'd like to admit.

The word on the street

This is the city that formed the backdrop to some of Ireland's defining events, including the Easter Rising of 1916, and that fathered such cultural icons as James Joyce, Samuel Beckett, Brendan Behan and U2. Dublin was once the most important city after London in an empire on which the sun never set – and it still has the architecture to prove it. Dublin's history is written in its streets, from the shell-scarred pillars of the General Post Office to the rejuvenated alleys of Temple Bar, not to mention the church spires and building cranes that punctuate the city's skyline.

Dubliners

Dublin's citizens are still coming to terms with the changes thrust upon them since the economic and cultural renaissance of the 1990s. House prices have risen beyond the means of many residents, local haunts have been tarted up into tourist honey-pots and the streets are filled with map-clutching newcomers. Yet, despite it all, Dubliners retain that civilized grace and ironic, self-deprecating humour that have seen the city through so many hard times. For all the weighty history and the shiny new street life, it is the people of Dublin who remain the city's greatest asset.

Drinking it in

No visit to Dublin would be complete without spending time in some of the city's 1,000-plus pubs. A Dublin pub is an excellent place to experience the *craic* – that quintessentially Irish sense of bonhomie that improves as the evening wears on and the glasses empty. Dublin has pubs to suit every taste, from Victorian gems to 21st-century wannabes, elegant lounge bars to spit-and-sawdust dives. There are bars for the early morning and the late night, for listening to music or watching the big match, for soaking up literary history or indulging in quiet conversation; bars for a quick tipple, a long lunch or a whole evening's drinking.

At a glance

Grafton Street and around

This area is the centre of tourist Dublin. It is home to many of the most significant sights, some wonderful arts and crafts shops and the city's best dining venues. Here, too, is the centre of government and Dublin's classiest and most expensive accommodation. The streets still retain much of their Georgian character, and away from the main drag are appealing cafés, designer boutiques, street markets and lively pubs. At the heart of it all is St Stephen's Green, a pleasant park that provides a haven from the city's bustle.

Temple Bar and around

Temple Bar lies north west of Grafton Street on the banks of the Liffey. Its ancient streets are a mixture of naff 'Oirishness' and creative modern artistry. Twenty years ago alternative types moved into this run-down district to set up art studios, second-hand shops, cheap restaurants, music stores and more. With state funding, the streets were tidied up, glittering cultural centres were built and rents soared. Now bohemia is smothered under designer bars, tourist hostels and organic markets. For the young at heart on a quick visit, this is the place to be: Temple Bar rocks at night with live music pouring out of every pub. On the edge of the district, history buffs will find plenty of interest at Christchurch Cathedral, City Hall and Dublin Castle, and children will get a buzz from Dublinia. There are rich pickings for culture vultures in the area's eclectic galleries, while a host of eateries, ranging from grab-and-go joints to stylish modern Irish restaurants, offer the most varied dining in the city.

The Liberties and west

South and west of the immediate city centre is an odd mishmash of areas, loosely defined as the Liberties. Major sights include St Patrick's Cathedral, Marsh's Library and the glitzy Guinness

Storehouse, which offers the best views in Dublin and a 'free' pint of beer. Further west is the Irish Museum of Modern Art and unmissable Kilmainham Gaol. Apart from these major attractions, the area is defined by street markets, modest housing and council estates. The Liberties have barely been touched by the Celtic Tiger phenomenon and probably never will be, now that the creature's a bit on the mangy side.

Ballsbridge and south

Ballsbridge and its surrounding suburbs are the poshest parts of Dublin and home to the city's well-heeled masses. Architecturally the area is characterized by grand Victorian and Edwardian terraces that ooze respectability and provide a welcome source of quality, non-hotel accommodation for visitors. Ballsbridge has good bus and DART connections to the city centre and the southern coastal villages, and, lately, has also developed a cultural identity of its own with good restaurants and some lively bars. To the north is the Grand Canal, where you can enjoy some pleasant walks, and the old Jewish quarter, which has a worthy museum.

O'Connell Street and around

Although it's less tourist orientated than areas south of the river, O'Connell Street has much to offer the visitor thanks to its powerful historical associations and impressive literary connections. You can still see bullet marks on the walls of the General Post Office from the Easter Rising of 1916, or trace Leopold Bloom's perambulations around the city on a Joyce-related walking tour (p232). O'Connell Street itself is one of the city's oldest and grandest boulevards, now cluttered with shop signs and statuary, but worth a stroll for its fine architecture. Nearby are the Dublin City Gallery, with its collection of modern art, the Dublin Writers' Museum and the James Joyce Centre. You'll also find much of the city's least expensive accommodation in this area, plus Dublin's oldest department stores and a lively street market.

From Smithfield to the Phoenix Park

Northwest of the Liffey is a relatively unvisited area of the city with a long history, an ancient church, the city's Four Courts and Smithfield market. Further west still are the old Collins Barracks, now housing a branch of the National Museum, and, beyond that again, the Phoenix Park, the largest enclosed public space in Europe. Within the park are Áras an Uachtaráin (the home of the Irish president), Dublin Zoo (home to assorted wildlife) and Ashtown Castle, a tiny early-17th-century house that was once home to ancestors of the nationalist leader Daniel O'Connell.

Glasnevin and Clontarf

The northern suburbs of the city have plenty of inexpensive B&Bs, making them a good accommodation option for the budget traveller. Other visitors can enjoy a lovely riverside walk through the remains of the city's industrial past in Clontarf and explore the final resting place of many of the 20th century's major players in Glasnevin's vast cemetery. Close by are the National Botanic Gardens, a wonderful horticultural showcase that will inspire green-fingered visitors.

Around Dublin

One of the best things about Dublin is its proximity to the coast and the countryside. Visitors can slip out of the city with ease to explore the Wicklow Hills or the shores of Dublin Bay. To the north is the coastal village of Howth, plus the long sandy beaches of Malahide and Skerries, and to the south are the old Victorian seaside towns of Dun Laoghaire and Bray with their stony beaches and imposing seafront walks. In addition to magnificent clifftop views, wildlife lovers will marvel at the teeming birdlife to be seen all along this coast. Further afield, the astonishing Newgrange passage tomb in County Meath is worth a day's excursion as part of anyone's Dublin itinerary for its ancient aura and evocative Neolithic carvings.

Ten of the best

Best

1 **Guinness Storehouse** Enjoy a panoramic view over the city and a perfect pint of Guinness in this stunningly converted brewery building, p54.

2 **National Museum of Archaeology and History** Viking hoards and memories of the 1916 uprising make this the most impressive museum in Dublin, p37.

3 **A night at the Cobblestone** Enjoy excellent Irish music and a convivial atmosphere at this Smithfield pub, p157.

4 **Christchurch Cathedral** Dublin's oldest building has medieval floor tiles, ancient tombstones and a host of treasures in the crypt, p52 .

5 **National Gallery of Ireland** This gallery provides a visitor-friendly introduction to Irish art as well as displaying an array of international masterpieces, p38.

6 **National Museum of Decorative Arts and History** Engrossing exhibitions at the former Collins Barracks bring to life the cultural history of Ireland, p77.

7 **Temple Bar** Make the most of this area's lively atmosphere, great shopping, groovy galleries, varied restaurants and buzzing nightlife, p46.

8 **Kilmainham Gaol** This hugely atmospheric site is where some of Ireland's brightest and best were confined during the 19th and 20th centuries, p55.

9 **1916 Rebellion Tour** This hysterical historical tour of the city is an excellent way to get to grips with one of Dublin's most important events, p29.

10 **Cliff walk at Bray** Escape the city and enjoy a breath of fresh air on this glorious coastal walk. The views of Dublin Bay are truly memorable, p95.

The ★ symbol is used throughout the book to indicate recommended sights.

Trip planner

Although Ireland's weather can be unpredictable – be prepared for both drizzle in July and brilliant winter sunshine in December – it is rarely extreme, and the mild climate ensures that a trip to Dublin is a pleasant experience at any time of year. Having said that, the city's laid-back street vibe is at its best between April and October, when the nights are long, the calendar is littered with festivals, pubs spill out onto the streets and Dublin's green spaces are draped with city workers and visitors. Summer temperatures in the city average a modest 15-20°C, while winter values rarely drop below 5-10°C.

Accommodation costs tend to increase in the high season of July and August, when the need to make reservations for rooms and even restaurant tables becomes paramount. You should also expect crowds in the city for St Patrick's Day and on Six Nations rugby weekends in February and March.

A day in Dublin

Begin your day with a full Irish breakfast, guaranteed to slow you down to the Irish pace of life for a few hours at least. Spend the morning marvelling at the collection of gold in the National Museum, followed by a quick gawk at the Picasso in the National Gallery and a really classy lunch at The Commons. In the afternoon stroll around the shops and alleys of Temple Bar before hopping on a bus to the Guinness Storehouse to enjoy a bird's-eye view of the city – and a pint of Guinness to boot.

In the evening head back to Temple Bar to sample modern Irish cuisine at Eden. After dinner enjoy a drink at Oliver St John Gogarty's, where you've a good chance of catching some traditional Irish music, or grab a cab over to the Brazen Head, Dublin's oldest bar. The next port of call for nightowls should be Harcourt Street, where the clubs get going around 2300. Chocolate Bar, POD and the Red Box are the hippest joints in town.

A weekend in Dublin

Start the second day of your stay in Dublin with a visit to Trinity College, where you can wander around the pretty quadrangle and peer at the Book of Kells in the old library building. For lunch, try one of the nearby cafés, such as the tiny Steps of Rome, followed in the afternoon by some serious retail therapy around Grafton Street. Christchurch Cathedral, Dublin Castle, St Patrick's Cathedral and O'Connell Street are all within walking distance if you're keen to do more sightseeing. Your evening could be enjoyably spent making the most of Dublin's cultural life at the Abbey or the Gate theatres, preceded by an exemplary early dinner at Chapter One.

If you've managed to squeeze a couple more days into your 'weekend', make the most of any fine weather by exploring the Phoenix Park. *Ryan's* or *Nancy Hands* on Parkgate Street are good options for lunch. In the afternoon cross the river to reach Kilmainham Gaol and the Irish Museum of Modern Art, or visit the National Museum of Decorative Arts and History at Collins Barracks. Spend the evening enjoying trad Irish music at the Cobblestone or hanging out at Voodoo.

A week in Dublin

With a few more days at your disposal, you should venture outside the city to the spectacular passage tomb at Newgrange or to the coastal towns of Dun Laoghaire and Howth. Have lunch at The Queen's in Dalkey to set you up for a walk around the cliffs at Bray.

In town, other worthwhile attractions include Prospect Cemetery, the Custom House, the Chester Beatty Library, Marsh's Library, not to mention the alcohol-preserved artefacts at the Natural History Museum and the mummified bodies at St Michan's Church. Take some time to wander the streets, admiring Dublin's beautiful Georgian architecture, or get to grips with the city's turbulent history on the 1916 Rebellion Tour. In the evening, try one of the comedy nights at the Ha'penny Bridge, the International, the Sugar Club or GUBU.

Step to the beat
The challenge for both locals and visitors is to stay in time and in tune with the rhythms of this fast-changing city.

Contemporary Dublin

Older than the Vikings but with one of the most youthful populations in Europe, Dublin is a city where the past and the present rub shoulders in striking proximity. A European business centre with enough time for long lunches and a serious dedication to the craic, Dublin will delight you with its roguish charm. The first-time visitor has an embarrassment of riches to discover, without even stepping into the tourist lures of Temple Bar, from bullet-riddled architecture in O'Connell Street to giant gas braziers towering above open-air concerts in Smithfield. There are artworks by Picasso and Caravaggio in the National Gallery, a ton of Celtic gold in the National Museum and mummified bodies in St Michan's Church. You can take to the river in a converted army amphibious vehicle, hop aboard the ghostbus on one of the city's sillier tours or catch the DART to Dun Laoghaire past wildlife habitats and seaside villages that have joined the commuter belt. The shops of Dublin are filled with beautiful Irish crafts and quality Irish-designed clothes or, if you prefer, funny green hats, Roy Keane T-shirts and tea towels with bad Irish jokes on them. Restaurants range from the too-familiar fast-food chains through gorgeously overdesigned café-bars to posh nouvelle Irish eateries with Michelin stars. And the pubs! From Edwardian splendour to unreconstructed 1960s chipboard, and joke 'paddywhackery' to postmodern glamour, this city has an astonishing glut of drinking dens to suit all comers.

Dublin's dedication to giving its visitors a good time creates an ever-changing city that alters so fast that even its most determined residents can hardly keep up. Nicknamed the 'Celtic Tiger', Ireland's unprecedented economic growth right through the 1990s utterly transformed this former poor relation of Europe. Dublin has expanded and grown wealthy to such an extent that people who have lived in the city all their lives struggle to recognize it. For decades Dublin's architecture reflected its economic and cultural decline; now the city's new wealth and pride is imprinted on its streets. A whole area of run-down docklands has sprouted acres of green glass to become the International Financial Services Centre, while new bridges arch across the river helping to break down the old distinction between wealthy south Dublin and run-down north Dublin. Young, well-educated Dubliners who might once have dreamed of a green card to the States now have cash to burn and little time to burn it in. They rent riverside apartments built on the ruins of the city's docklands, eat and drink at designer café-bars that come in and out of fashion quicker than a reality TV pop star, and buy second homes in Spain or the far west of Ireland.

To meet the needs of this burgeoning new Dublin, thousands of foreign workers have arrived in the city, shockingly quickly for a largely monocultural community. Where other capitals have slowly absorbed waves of immigrants and benefited from their diversity, Dublin seems bewildered by the sudden influx of foreign arrivals, and not all native Dubliners are coping with their new neighbours. The situation is not helped by the unpalatable fact that the Irish economy has begun to slow down since the heady days of the 1990s, with daily news stories of job losses and cutbacks in government spending. For the ignorant minority this has become the rationale for a dislike of non-Irish cultures. The newspapers carry stories of attacks on foreigners and even long-term, non-native residents are experiencing antagonism.

Dublin has found itself suddenly and violently jerked out of the life it knew for decades, and into a world of wealthy twenty-somethings, sad-eyed refugees and fun-hungry tourists; new buildings stand where ruins once quietly mouldered, and revelations about the priesthood, about brown envelope-wielding politicians and crooked property developers have shaken old beliefs and securities. For all the new developments, there have been few improvements in the city's inadequate transport system, and while a projected new tramway may do much to alleviate the problem, for the moment the rush hour barely stops before it starts again, there are traffic jams in mid-morning along the quays and just getting across the city is an adventure for pedestrians. Meanwhile, the Georgian streets, medieval cathedrals and the even more ancient river quietly wonder at all the fuss, while out in the suburbs ordinary Dubliners sit in their bars and living rooms shaking their heads at every new building project, every tribunal investigating another political scandal, every luxury hotel replacing a bank or a horse fair or a school.

Dublin carries its history, its culture and its feelings on its sleeve for all to admire. Come here for the music, the food, the *craic*, the history and above all for that mouthy, politically incorrect, jackeen humour that simmers just below the surface and can break out in the oddest places. For the real voice of Dublin, listen to the taxi man who brings you from the airport, the bus driver endlessly dealing with map-wielding tourists, the dinner-jacketed waiter in one of the city's older restaurants, or the stall-holder selling fruit and veg in Moore Street market.

Dublin is easily and cheaply accessible from most British airports and from an increasing number of European cities. An alternative, especially if you intend to travel beyond Dublin, is to take one of the many high-speed car ferries that shuttle across the Irish Sea from Liverpool and Holyhead. There are long-haul direct flights from the USA and Canada, but no direct flights from Australia or the Far East; instead travellers from these countries should fly to London and make a connection there.

Public transport around Dublin is slow but reliable. Buses cover the city and its suburbs, while the DART and suburban rail network provide a good service to outlying towns. Avoid trying to drive around the city by car, and if you're brave enough to cycle, be aware that you may have a problem securing your bike when you're not using it. Fortunately, one of Dublin's best features is its small size, and walking is often the quickest and most enjoyable way to reach your destination. Guided walking tours of the city are an excellent way of getting to know Dublin's history and layout.

Getting there

Air

From the UK **Aer Lingus**, **British Airways**, **Cityjet**, **Easyjet**
(including Go flights) and **Ryanair** all offer frequent services into
Dublin from most of Britain's major cities. Smaller airlines offer less
regular flights from other locations. All the airlines keep a keen eye
on one another's rates, and there are very good offers to be found
if you are prepared to fly off peak and mid-week; Ryanair often has
the cheapest deals. Expect to pay anything from £11 mid-week on
a special offer to around £100 at peak times. All the airlines offer an
online booking facility. Before you book your flight, check the price
of a return compared to a single. Sometimes it can be cheaper to
get two single flights, especially if you are paying in sterling in one
direction and euros in the other. Prices go up in summer and for
other holiday periods, so book well in advance if you want to travel
at these times. Flight time to Dublin from London is about an hour;
less from most other UK cities.

From Europe **AB Airlines**, **Adria Airways**, **Aer Lingus**,
Aeroflot, **Air France**, **Alitalia**, **Iberia**, **Lufthansa**, **Maersk**,
Ryanair and **SAS** offer regular flights from most European
cities into Dublin. Typical fares are €49 one-way from Paris;
€74 one-way from Milan; €99 one-way from Rome. Flight times
vary but are likely to be upwards of two hours.

From North America **Aer Lingus**, **TWA**, **United Airlines**
and **Virgin Atlantic** offer regular flights from major US cities to
Dublin. Direct services on Aer Lingus depart from Baltimore ($179
one way), Boston ($149 one way), New York ($149 one way), Los
Angeles ($234 one way) and Chicago ($209 one way). Flights from
the west coast of the USA can be very expensive and travellers may
get a better deal by flying to London and taking a budget flight to
Dublin from there. Flights from Canada are usually via London.

→ Airlines and discount travel agents

Airlines

Aer Lingus T 0845 084 4444 (UK), www.aerlingus.ie
Air Canada T 1888 247 2262 (CA), www.aircanada.com
Air France T 0820 820 820 (FR), www.airfrance.com
Alitalia T 8488 65 642 (ITA), www.alitalia.com
British Airways T 0845 773 3377 (UK), www.britishairways.com
British Midland T 0870 607 0555 (UK), www.flybmi.com
Cityjet T 01 870 0100 (IRE), www.cityjet.com
Delta Airlines T 1800 241 4141 (USA), www.delta.com
Easyjet T 0870 600 0000 (UK), www.easyjet.com
Lufthansa T 01805 838 4267 (GER), www.lufthansa.com
Maersk Air T 7010 7474 (DEN), www.maersk-air.com
Northwest Airlines T 1800 447 4747 (USA), www.nwa.com
Ryanair T 0871 246 0000 (UK), www.ryanair.com
Virgin Atlantic T 1800 862 8621 (USA), www.virginatlantic.com

Discount travel agents

www.airbrokers.com
www.cheapflights.com
www.expedia.com
www.sta-travel.com
www.trailfinders.com
www.travelcuts.com

Airport information Dublin International Airport, **T** 01 814 1111, is located 12 km (eight miles) north of the city. Facilities at the arrivals hall include cash machines, car hire desks (p210), left luggage facilities (daily 0600-2300), a Dublin Tourism office (daily 0800-2200) and a CIE counter that provides information about onward bus services. The departures hall has assorted shops, bars and cafés. There's also a branch of the Bank of Ireland, where you can change money during banking hours, as well as a post office at car park level.

There is no train service between the airport and the city centre but Dublin Bus runs two Airlink Express buses: the 747 service stops at Parnell Square West, O'Connell Street, Busáras and the airport; the 748 service connects Tara Street DART station, Heuston Station, Connolly Station, Busáras and the airport. The fare for both routes is €4.50 adult single, €7.50 adult return, child €2 single. Rambler tickets (p26) are also valid on the Airlink service. The 747 runs every 10 to 15 minutes from 0545 (0715 on Sun) to midnight daily, while the 748 runs about every 30 minutes from 0650 (0700 on Sun) to 2100. Journey time is about 35 minutes, but can be significantly longer in the rush hour. Local buses 41, 41A and 41B also serve the airport. The journey takes an hour and the single fare is €1.40.

A private Aircoach leaves the airport every 15 minutes from 0500 to midnight and then hourly from midnight to 0500. It travels directly to O'Connell Street and then continues on a circuit through south Dublin city centre and Ballsbridge, dropping off at designated stops beside the major hotels. The fare is €6 single, €10 return. Accompanied children travel for free.

Taxis cost around €20 from the airport to the city centre; slightly less from the city to the airport. A cab can be the most convenient transport option, but is expensive unless three or four people share the ride and the fare.

Car
Motorways links Dublin with Dundalk in the north (M1), Maynooth in the west (M4) and Kildare in the south (M7). Beyond these destinations major roads vary in quality, and driving can be slow in rural areas. Driving is on the left and speed limits vary from 70 mph (110 kph) on motorways to 60 mph (91 kph) on open roads and 30 mph (50 kph) in built-up areas. Distances on road signs are usually given in kilometres, but speed limits are given in miles per

hour. Place names are always given in Gaelic and English. Fuel is significantly cheaper in the Republic than in the UK: unleaded petrol costs around €0.88 per litre. For details of car hire firms in the city, see p210. You should book your hire vehicle in advance, particularly in the summer months.

Coach

Bus Éireann (p218) runs a network of comprehensive bus routes between most towns and cities in the Republic and Northern Ireland. Tickets can be purchased on the day or in advance from bus stations. Discounted fares are available if you purchase an Irish Rover or Emerald Card ticket, which allow unlimited travel on bus or rail for three, five, eight or 15 days.

Sea

Four main ferry companies offer car ferry services between the British mainland and Dublin. **Irish Ferries**, **T** 08075 171717 (UK), **T** 890 313 1131 (Ireland), www.irishferries.com, and **Stena Line**, **T** 0870 570 7070 (UK), **T** 01 204 777 (Ireland), www.stenaline.com, both offer a service between Holyhead and Dublin Port (3¼ hours), with Stena Line also running another high-speed service between Holyhead and Dun Laoghaire (1 hour 40 minutes). **P&O**, **T** 0870 2424 777 (UK), **T** 1800 409 049 (Ireland), www.poirishsea.com, and **Seacat**, **T** 08705 523 523 (UK), www.seacat.co.uk, both offer crossings from Liverpool to Dublin. The Seacat is significantly faster (3¾ hours) than the P&O ferry (7½ hours). Dublin Port is in the city and accessible by bus 53 from Busáras or on special buses laid on by the ferry companies themselves. Dun Laoghaire is 30-minutes' drive south of Dublin and easily reached on the DART.

A return fare for four adults plus car in peak season costs between £300 and £400, but travelling at off-peak times or within time limits brings the price down, and remember that you'll save the cost of car hire in Ireland. You should also check the ferry companies' websites for special fare offers, which may include hotel accommodation. Before deciding to travel to Dublin by ferry however, you should take into account the crossing time, as well as the cost of meals and drinks on board. You should also be aware that the Irish Sea can be very rough during the winter months and that services may be cancelled altogether in severe weather.

Travelling as a foot passenger on a combined coach/ferry or train/ferry ticket can be good value although it obviously takes much longer than a flight. Enquire at a travel agent for details.

Train

Iarnród Éireann (p218) is the national rail provider. Trains are the swiftest means of getting between Dublin and other towns in Ireland, although they are generally more expensive than buses and cover far fewer destinations. Tickets can be booked online.

Dublin has two intercity railway stations: **Connolly Station** on Amiens Street, **T** 01 836 3333, serves Belfast, Derry, Sligo and Roslaire. There are around eight trains a day to Belfast and the journey takes about two hours. **Heuston Station** on St John's Road West, **T** 01 836 5421, serves Cork, Galway, Westport, Tralee, Killarney, Limerick, Wexford and Waterford and other destinations in the south and west of the country. Connolly Station is on the DART line and bus 90 runs between the two stations.

Getting around

Bus

Local buses, run by **Dublin Bus** (p218), are frequent and cheap . Bus stops are green with a sign indicating the bus numbers that stop there. There should also be a timetable on display but this tends to get vandalised, so don't depend on it to plan your journey. Fares start at €0.75 for a short hop within the city (up to three stages), and the exact amount must be paid in coins to the driver on boarding the bus. The driver can only give change in the form of a ticket, which can be redeemed at the Dublin Bus office on O'Connell Street. An excellent bus map of the city is available free of charge from Dublin Bus or the tourist office.

If you plan to stay in Dublin for more than 24 hours and you intend to travel around the city a lot, you should consider buying a Rambler ticket, valid for one (€4.50), three, five or seven (€16.50) consecutive days on all Dublin Bus scheduled services including the Airlink bus (but not for travel on Nitelink buses, ferry services or bus tours).

Nitelink buses run every night from Monday to Saturday along 21 routes from the city centre to outlying districts. Westbound services depart from Westmoreland Street, northbound buses from D'Olier Street and southbound buses from College Street. The service begins at 0030 and continues at 20-minute intervals until 0200 from Monday to Wednesday and until 0430 from Thursday to Saturday. Fares are €4 for shorter journeys, €6 for longer ones. Pre-paid tickets can be bought at the departure points.

Car

Although car hire outlets are dotted all over Dublin (p210), driving is not the most relaxing means of getting around the city centre. During the day parking is very limited, and movement across the city, even outside the rush hours, is slow. Once you escape the city limits, however, driving is a much less stressful experience. Parking is available in both multi-storey car parks (spaces are indicated on signboards around the city) or on the street by purchasing and displaying a ticket from roadside machines. Few hotels have their own car parks but some have allocated spaces in private car parks.

Cycling

Cycling in Dublin is not for the faint-hearted: traffic is heavy; there are no cycle lanes; every railing has signs prohibiting the parking of bikes; there are few dedicated cycle racks, and if you leave your bike unattended, any removable parts are likely to be stolen in your absence. If you're still determined to explore Dublin by pedal power, bear in mind that there are no bike hire facilities in the city, so you'll have to bring your own wheels.

Taxi

Taxis were deregulated in Dublin in 2002. There are now far more cabs available, but this does not seem to have resulted in fare reductions. Taxi ranks in the city centre are situated at O'Connell Street Upper, St Stephen's Green, Aston Quay and College Green as well as at Busáras and the railway stations. Licensed cabs run on a meter which starts at €2.75 and goes up by €0.20 for each ninth of a mile or 30-second period. There are additional charges for each extra passenger, for each piece of luggage, for a call out, for travelling on Sundays and for travelling after 2200 on other days. Unlicensed cabs tend to charge a flat fee to your destination, which should be negotiated in advance. See also p216.

Train

Dublin's light railway system, the **DART** (Dublin Area Rapid Transit) links the coastal suburbs with the city centre. It is useful for short hops between the north and the south of the city and for transport to hotels and places of interest in some suburban areas. The system operates from Howth and Malahide in the north to Greystones, County Wicklow, in the south. It is supplemented by the Northern Suburban Line to Dundalk, the Southern Suburban Line to Arklow, the Western Suburban Line between Connolly Station and Mullingar and the Arrow Line from Heuston Station to Kildare. The trains are clean and fast but get very crowded during the rush hours. Note that bikes are not permitted on the DART. Tickets can be bought from all DART stations or from the Rail Travel Centre at 35 Abbey Street Lower. A Short Hop ticket provides unlimited travel on Dublin Bus, suburban rail and DART services for a single day; Four-Day Explorer and Weekly Short Hop tickets are also available.

Walking

This is the best way to see the city. By exploring on foot you'll gain an insight into the city's layout and get a vibrant impression of Dublin's street life; you may even make some new friends as you wait endlessly to cross the city's busy roads. Grafton Street, Henry Street and parts of Temple Bar are pedestrianized, but in the rest of the city you'll have to negotiate heavy traffic with only some disorganized traffic signals to help you.

Most of the major sights south of the river, including Dublin Castle, Trinity College, the cathedrals, the National Museum, Grafton Street and St Stephen's Green, are 10-minutes' walk or less from Temple Bar. Sights north of the river are mostly within five to 10-minutes' walk of O'Connell Street, although it takes rather longer to reach Smithfield. All but the most dedicated walkers will want to catch a bus to reach Phoenix Park, Kilmainham and sights further afield.

Tours

An excellent way to get an insight into the city is to join one of the many specialist guided bus or walking tours doing the rounds of Dublin's familiar and not-so-familiar sites of historical and cultural interest. These usually run daily and can be joined at the starting point, although it is wise to book ahead for some of the more unusual walking tours, as they may not run if there isn't enough interest.

Bus tours

Dublin Bus operates the hop-on, hop-off *Dublin City Tour*, with open-top buses running every 10 minutes between 0930 and 1700 and every 30 minutes from 1700 to 1830, starting at McDonalds on O'Connell Bridge. The complete tour takes over an hour and visits 16 sights around the city, with guided commentary provided by the bus driver. The bus ticket (€10 adult, €5 child under 14) includes discounts at each of the sights and is valid for a day. You can join the tour at any point along the route, and break your journey at any stage to explore a particular attraction. Dublin Bus also runs a *Coast and Castle Tour*, which takes in the Botanic Gardens, the Casino at Marino and Malahide Castle before heading back in to the city via Howth and Dollymount Strand. Tickets (€17 adult, €8.50 child) include a tour of Malahide Castle.

Guide Friday, 13 South Leinster Street, **T** 01 676 5377, offers a hop-on, hop-off city tour similar to the Dublin Bus route, but leaves out Kilmainham Gaol and the National Museum of Modern Art. Ticket prices (€12 adult, €4 child, €28 family) include discounted admission to several sights for the duration of your trip.

Dublin Ghostbus Tour, **T** 01 873 4222, is a two-hour story-telling tour that runs twice nightly at 1900 and 2130 from Tuesday to Friday. It starts from 59 O'Connell Street and takes in haunted houses, bodysnatching, Dublin's association with Dracula and Irish wakes. The tour costs €20 per person and is considered unsuitable for children.

Walking tours

Walk Macabre, **T** 087 677 1512, www.ghostwalk.cjb.com, runs daily tours focussing on the many horror writers who lived and wrote in Dublin. The tours start at 1930 from the main gates to St Stephen's Green and last 1½ hours. Tickets (€7-9) must be booked in advance by phone or from Dublin Tourism.

Starting from the pedestrian entrance to Dublin Castle on Dame Street, the *Zozimus Ghostly Experience*, **T** 01 661 8646, www.zozimus.com, leads visitors on a spooky walk around medieval Dublin. The tour lasts 1½ hrs and usually begins at 1900 in winter and at 2100 in summer, although times should be confirmed. Tickets for the tour cost €8 and advance booking is essential.

Our favourite guided walk is the two-hour *1916 Rebellion Tour*, **T** 01 676 2493, 1916@indigo.ie, which describes and analyzes the events that took place at the trouble hotspots during Easter 1916. The tour only runs between April and September, setting off from the International Bar on Wicklow Street at 1130 from Tuesday to Saturday and at 1230 on Sunday. Tickets cost €7.

A comprehensive survey of Dublin's history right up to the Good Friday peace process is provided on the *Historical Walking Tour of Dublin*, **T** 01 878 0227, www.historicalinsights.ie, which starts from the gates of Trinity College. There are two tours daily at 1100 and 1500 between May and September, and a single tour at 1200 on Fridays, Saturdays and Sundays from October to April. Tickets are €10 and you can pay on the day.

For lots of drinking and reciting, plus a literary quiz, join the *Literary Pub Crawl*, **T** 01 670 5602, www.dublinpubcrawl.com, which kicks off from the Duke pub on Duke Street. The crawl takes place at 1930 Monday to Saturday and at 1200 and 1930 on Sunday from Easter to the end of October, and at 1930 Thursday to Saturday in winter. It lasts 2½ hours and costs €7.90 per person.

Tourist information

Dublin Tourism, St Andrew's Church, Suffolk St, **T** 01 605 7700, www.visitdublin.com *Sep-Jun, Mon-Sat 0900-1730, Jul and Aug, Mon-Sat 0830-1900, Sun 1000-1500.* A sight in itself, St Andrew's church houses the most central and most useful of several tourist offices around the city. Services include accommodation advice and bookings, ferry and concert tickets, a car hire desk, bureau de change, loads of free leaflets and some city-wide and Irish guide books for sale. There is also a good café upstairs. Elsewhere, the handiest office is at 14 O'Connell Street Upper (*Mon-Sat 0900-1700*), which is often less crowded than the Suffolk Street branch. Other branches are at Baggot Street Bridge (*Mon-Fri 0930-1200 and 1230-1700*), Dun Laoghaire Ferry Terminal (*Mon-Sat 1000-1800*) and at Dublin Airport (*daily 0800-2200*).

Grafton Street and around 33 The city's political and commercial heart has museums, shops, galleries and a much-loved park.

Temple Bar and around 46 A 14th-century setting for Dublin's 21st-century culture: cyber cafés, art galleries, packed pubs and cool clubs, watched over by a castle and a cathedral.

The Liberties and west 53 Old-style Dublin has St Patrick's Cathedral and the Guinness Brewery on its doorstep, with modern art and an infamous 19th-century gaol nearby.

Ballsbridge and south 58 The Grand Canal and the former Jewish quarter separate the centre from this well-to-do suburb of hotels and guesthouses.

O'Connell Street and around 62 This grand old boulevard has seen better days, but is still rich in historical and literary associations.

From Smithfield to the Phoenix Park 76 A museum in a former barracks, a displaced horse fair and a vast green retreat where deer still roam.

Glasnevin and Clontarf 82 These suburbs hold the city's botanic gardens and a famous cemetery.

Grafton Street and around

This area has been at the heart of Dublin since Viking times, when
College Green *formed the city's public meeting ground.* **Trinity**
College *was established here in the late 16th century followed by
the Irish Parliament in the 18th century. In the same period, the upper
classes created a new residential district in the countryside south of
the river, constructing grand houses, elegant streets, pretty squares
and Georgian terraces that still characterize the area. Later, the
Victorians chose this part of the city for their most grandiose public
buildings, including two* **National Museums** *and the* **National**
Gallery*, and it was here that, after a century of decay, the Celtic Tiger
first began to flex its claws. The streets are now dominated by offices,
government buildings, hotels, pubs and restaurants, as well as some
of the city's most significant sights. Also here is* **Leinster House***, the
home of the Irish Parliament.* **Grafton Street** *itself is a pedestrian
shopping zone bustling with department stores, flower stalls, buskers,
tourists and giggling gangs of Euro kids.*

▸▸ *See Sleeping p106, Eating and drinking p127, Bars and clubs p149*

 Sights

★ Trinity College
College Green, **T** 01 608 2320, www.tcd.ie *Mon-Sat 0930-1700.
Closed for 10 days at Christmas. All cross city buses.* *Map 2, A8, p249*

Trinity College was founded in 1592 by Elizabeth I, who hoped that
a Protestant university would stop the young and restless of the
Pale wandering off to Europe to be seduced by the old religion.
Former students include Oscar Wilde, Samuel Beckett, Jonathan
Swift, Mary Robinson and Mary MacAleese, the current President
of Ireland. Women were first admitted in 1903, but Catholics were
all-but forbidden by their church from studying here until 1970.

Walking through the entrance gate of the college is rather like passing through the wardrobe into Narnia. Outside, the traffic junction of College Green has the highest casualty rate of any in Dublin, but inside the road rage and jaywalking give way instantly to a world of clipped grass, Georgian architecture and ivory towers. Dominating the quadrangle is the campanile, with a Henry Moore statue, *Reclining Connected Forms*, beside it. On the left and right flanks are the chapel and the examination hall, while to the far right is the **Old Library**, built between 1712 and 1732, and home to the Book of Kells Exhibition. In front of the Arts and Social Sciences building is the *Sphere within a Sphere* sculpture, while inside you'll find the **Douglas Hyde Gallery** (*Mon, Wed, Fri 1100-1600, Thu 1100-1900, Sat 1100-1645, free*), which hosts modern art exhibitions. Also here is the **Dublin Experience** (*late May-early Oct, daily 1000-1700, €4.20*) a 45-minute audio-visual introduction to the history of the city, from Viking times to the present day. You might also want to check out the Gothic old museum building to the east of the Old Library, which now houses a collection of geological bric-a-brac.

Book of Kells Exhibition

Old Library Building, Trinity College, **T** 01 608 2308. *Mon-Sat 0930-1700, Sun 0930-1430. All cross city buses. Map 2, B8, p249*

You can find your way to the Book of Kells Exhibition without the aid of a map: just follow the tour groups. It is situated in what was once an open colonnade in the Old Library. Beyond the assorted paraphernalia in the lobby – decorated tea towels, pot pourri and the like – the exhibition itself has lots of information about the context of the Book of Kells, its history, manufacture and artwork.

! Trinity College Library has over three million books in its collection. Since 1801 it has had the right to claim a copy of every book published in the United Kingdom and Ireland.

▶ Book of Kells

The Book of Kells was begun around AD 800 by the monks of St Colmcille's (Columba) monastery on the island of Iona, and kept at the monastery of Kells in County Meath for the following seven centuries. This illuminated manuscript of the four Gospels is one of the oldest books in the world and is characterized by elaborate full-page illustrations, exquisite drawings and heavily decorated initial letters. The book now has 680 pages, having lost 30 of its original opening and concluding folios during its turbulent history.

It first came to Dublin around 1653 through the efforts of Henry Cromwell, son of Oliver, and was rebound in 1661 into four volumes, one of which is now always on display in Trinity College, its pages turned regularly.

Most fascinating are the unintentional marks left behind by the monks who created the book: holes in the vellum where the artist has worked around the natural flaws; faint guidelines drawn to ensure the text was straight; hair follicles not quite removed when the skins were prepared, and the blank, unfinished folios 29v to 31r.

This exhibition is an excellent example of how accompanying material and information can improve and enhance the central feature, although, after seeing the magnified displays in the main gallery, the room containing the actual books can be a bit of a disappointment. However, it is noticeably less crowded, which means you can have a good stare at the tiny, intricate illustrations. Two pages of the Book of Kells are on display each day, alongside two other ancient texts from the library's collection.

Afterwards, wander upstairs to marvel at the magnificent 65 m Long Room, where around 200,000 of the library's oldest books are kept, alongside marble busts of notable academic and literary figures, and an Irish harp dating back to the 14th century.

Bank of Ireland

College Green, **T** 01 677 6801. *Mon-Fri 1000-1600 (Thu 1700). Free. Free tours of the House of Lords Tue 1030, 1130, 1345 (except bank holidays). All cross city buses. Map 2, A7, p249*

Just over College Green from Trinity is the Bank of Ireland building, a sweeping,18th-century Palladian edifice, which originally served as the Irish Houses of Parliament. The outside of the building, best viewed from College Green, has Corinthian and Ionic porticoes, statuary and a pretty cannon-filled piazza. It was started during the 18th century by Sir Edward Lovett Pearce, with work continuing under James Gandon and Richard Parke. The building was sold off to the bank in 1804, following the Act of Union, on the understanding that its interior would be gutted, leaving no trace of Irish independence as represented by the two parliamentary chambers. The House of Commons was remodelled accordingly, but the **House of Lords** remained intact and is now open to the public. Inside you will see the original fixtures and fittings carved out of Irish oak, and tapestries dating back to the 1730s depicting the triumph of William of Orange at the Battle of the Boyne; an event that would have been celebrated by the Anglo-Irish Protestant parliament that sat in this room.

Next door, the **Bank of Ireland Arts Centre** houses an exhibition entitled 'A Journey Through 200 Years of History' (*Tue-Fri 0930-1600. €1.50*). It's largely a naff sales pitch for the bank's potential teenage customers, but is worth a visit in order to see the original House of Commons' mace, and a letter from the Abbey Theatre (p170) that is signed by JM Synge, WB Yeats and Lady Gregory.

● *Between College Green and the top of Grafton Street, check out the buxom statue of Molly Malone, commonly known as the 'tart with the cart'. The subject of the famous Dublin ballad was a real-life 18th-century street trader, selling 'cockles and mussels alive, alive o'.*

★ National Museum of Archaeology and History

Kildare St, **T** 01 677 7444, www.museum.ie *Tue-Sat 1000-1700,
Sun 1400-1700. Free. Bus 7, 7A, 8 (from Burgh Quay), 10, 11, 13 (from
O'Connell St), DART Pearse St.   Map 2, C9, p249*

Of all the sights in this part of Dublin, the National Museum of
Archaeology and History is the star turn. For a start it is housed in
a beautiful purpose-built Victorian building, whose exterior and
lobby are sights in themselves.

Inside, the undisputed highlight of the museum's collection
is the stunning hoard of Bronze Age gold, which has turned
up over the decades in peat bogs, railway excavations and
ploughed fields. Look out especially for the Tara Brooch, the
Ardagh Chalice and the Loughnashade Trumpet. Guarding the
doorway to this treasure trove are two stone *sheela-na-gigs*, carved
female effigies with prominent genitalia, that formerly graced the
outer doors of Ireland's churches until they were removed by
prudish later generations.

Upstairs, Viking and medieval artefacts give an insight into the
development of Dublin, as well as revealing more of early Ireland's
obsession with precious metals. The 'Road to Independence'
exhibition is less enticing, however, with displays that are largely
limited to death masks, weapons and uniforms belonging to the
men who fought and died for Irish independence. Of most interest
in this section of the museum is the video archive charting Irish life
in the early 20th century.

● *Flanked by the National Museum and the National Library,
Leinster House (which houses the Irish Parliament) is worth a peer
through the railings. It was built in 1745 for the Earl of Kildare by the
architect Richard Castle and was designed with two entrances: the
one on Kildare Street has a typical Georgian town-house façade, while
the other on Merrion Square originally faced on to fields and so was
built in a country-house style.*

National Gallery: the Irish collection

Occupying a 15-square-metre space in the Shaw Room is the enormous 1854 *Marriage of Aoife and Strongbow* by Daniel Maclise, donated to the gallery in 1972. The wedding takes place amid much gnashing of teeth and rending of garments, but the central figures are less interesting than the attendant handmaidens who look distinctly as though they'd rather be anywhere else.

In the rooms that are dedicated to Irish painters look out for the *Opening of the Sixth Seal* by Francis Danby and *The Holy Well* by William Orpen. You will also see the original paintings of *A Connemara Girl* by Nicholas Burke and *Launching the Curragh* by Paul Henry, whose ubiquitous prints grace the corridors and bedrooms of countless three-star hotels all over the country.

★ National Gallery of Ireland

Merrion Square West, **T** 01 661 5133, www.nationalgallery.ie
Mon-Sat 0930-1730 (Thu 2030), Sun 1200-1730. Free guided tours Sat 1500 and Sun 1000, 1500, 1600. Free. Bus 5, 7, 7A (from Burgh Quay), 10 (from O'Connell St), 44, 48A (from Hawkins St), DART Pearse St (5-mins' walk). Map 2, C9, p249

The National Gallery (and its Millennium Wing) is home to art treasures from around the world, and is especially impressive when you consider that the collection was only started 150 years ago. The big names of European art are well represented, with works by Caravaggio, Degas, El Greco, Fra Angelico, Goya, Mantegna, Monet, Picasso, Rembrandt, Tintoretto, Titian, Velasquez and Vermeer. There is also a decent display of English art and a marvellous collection by Irish artists, who may be less well known to the average punter. Check out the Jack Yeats rooms and the 'Touching Art' multi-media guide, which lets you home in on details of one hundred or so works from the gallery's collection. In order to do the gallery justice, plan to spend a whole morning here, or take one of the free tours.

● *On the landing between Room 9 and the Shaw Room, look out for an installation featuring the profile of Gay Byrne, the long-serving and iconic TV host of the incomparable 'Late Late Show' on Friday nights on RTÉ1. Gay's profile is set on a background of wallpaper – a fitting tribute to the man who spent so many hours in so many Irish sitting rooms.*

National Museum of Natural History

Merrion St Upper, **T** 01 677 7444, www.museum.ie *Tue-Sat 1000-1700, Sun 1400-1700. Free. Bus 7, 7A, 8 (from Burgh Quay), DART Pearse St (5-mins' walk). Map 2, C9, p249*

Founded in 1857 when the Victorian mania for collecting was at its peak, this museum has changed very little since it was first established. Housed in the original 19th-century cabinets are long-dead creatures, some of which are examples of species that are now extinct. Standing guard over the displays are the 10,000-year-old skeletons of three giant elks.

Government offices

Merrion St Upper. *Free tours Sat 0900-1700 on the hour. Tickets from the foyer of the National Gallery. No pre-booking. Bus 7, 7A, 8 (from Burgh Quay), DART Pearse St (5-mins' walk). Map 2, D9, p249*

Not usually a place you'd associate with a leisure trip to Dublin, the government offices in Merrion Street, just down from the Natural History Museum, were extensively refurbished in the early 1990s to much furore in the press about the cost of it all. They are open for tours on Saturdays only and are worth the rigmarole of getting a ticket just to see what all the fuss was about. The tour is great fun, as long as you don't mind the security frisking at the entrance and

Political slant
Tour the Government offices on Merrion Street for an intriguing glimpse behind the scenes of Irish politics.

the men with head mikes who follow you around, making sure you don't swipe the silver or plant something nasty in one of the meeting rooms. The plush interior is divided into innumerable rooms, each named after the type of native Irish wood that dominates its décor. The Beech Room was used for the Irish part of the Good Friday peace negotiations, but the red stains on the carpet are allegedly due only to spilled wine. Test your knowledge of Irish history by identifying the portraits of politicians that hang around the place. All the big names are there; they just get shuffled about a bit depending on who's in power. Best of all is the Taoiseach's Room, where there are banks of ageing technology, reminiscent of the original Starship Enterprise, and a Blofeld-style lift to the helicopter pad on the roof: useful for a quick getaway

if a tribunal investigation uncovers something too hot to handle.

Merrion Square

Bus 5, 7, 7A (from Burgh Quay), 10 (from O'Connell St), 44, 48A (from Hawkins St), DART Pearse St (5 mins walk). Map 2, C/D10/11, p249

Construction of this near-perfect Georgian square began in 1762. On four sides, rows of elegant houses – many still bearing original door furniture, skylights and coal holes – surround quiet Ryan Park. A rash of plaques marks the houses where Dublin's rich and famous once lived: the Wilde family (No 1); Daniel O'Connell (No 58); WB Yeats (No 82); horror novelist Joseph Sheridan Le Fanu (No 70); George Russell, better known as the poet Æ (No 84), and the Nobel prize-winning scientist Erwin Schrodinger (No 65). Number 35 housed the British embassy until it was burned down in 1972 by angry protestors, demonstrating against the Bloody Sunday killings in Derry.

Oscar Wilde's former home at number one is now an English language school, but some of its downstairs rooms have been restored to their appearance in Oscar's day, and can be visited (*Mon, Wed and Thur 1015, 1115. €2.54*). However, unless you're a big Wilde fan, you'd do better to save your cash for 29 Fitzwilliam Street, which is a more comprehensive restoration project.

● *In the central garden of Merrion Square, look for the colourful and characterful statue of Oscar Wilde, lovingly known as the 'quare in the square' or the 'fag on the crag'.*

Number Twenty-Nine

29 Fitzwilliam St, **T** 01 702 6165, www.esb.ie/education *Tue-Sat 1000-1700, Sun 1400-1700. Closed for 2 weeks before Christmas. €3.15. Bus 7, 8, 10, 45, DART Pearse St. Map 2, D11, p249*

A collaborative effort between the electricity board and the National Museum of Ireland, this is a carefully restored Georgian town house filled with furnishings dating back to the late 18th century, including authentic carpets and knick-knacks. The house

★ Statues and monuments

Best

- Oscar Wilde in Merrion Square, p41
- James Kavanagh on the banks of the Grand Canal, p59
- Monument of Light on O'Connell Street, p66
- James Larkin on O'Connell Street, p66
- Famine sculpture on Custom House Quay, p76

provides a fine insight into middle-class life of the period, with a detailed account of the Beatty family and their servants, who lived at number 29 when it was first built. An informative audio-visual display is followed by the guided tour, which, despite the grandeur of the decor (and the modern central heating), makes it clear just how dark, cold and difficult to maintain these tall, narrow houses were. Water came in by cart, as did turf and coal, and sewage was carried away every few days. Mrs Beatty sold number 29 in 1806 at a profit of £380, just before a sharp decline in Dublin house prices, resulting from the 1800 Act of Union.

St Stephen's Green
Bus 10, 11, 13B, 20B, 27C, 46A/B, 84X, 127, 129, 746. Map 2, p249

Encompassing 27 acres, St Stephen's Green has had many incarnations over the centuries. Until the 1660s it was an expanse of open ground where people grazed their cattle and public executions took place. Then, as the surrounding area began to be developed, the green was partly fenced in and became a park. In 1814 the public were excluded from St Stephen's Green and only 'keyholders' (residents of the grand houses overlooking the park) could use it for an annual fee of one guinea. In 1877 Lord Ardilaun, one of the Guinness family, introduced a bill to Parliament making the green a public space once again, and personally put up the cash to turn it into a pleasure ground. Nowadays, St Stephen's

Knock knock

*Dublin's Georgian doors are an elegant reminder of the city's
18th-century heyday.*

Green remains the city's playground. It's a great place for a lazy picnic lunch, with regular concerts taking place here during the summer months.

The main entrance to the park, at the junction with Grafton Street, commemorates the Dublin Fusiliers who died fighting for the British in the Boer War; it is traditionally known by locals as 'traitors' gate'. At the opposite entrance is a statue of the Three Fates, donated by the German government in gratitude for the help and support provided by the Irish after the Second World War. In the north-west corner of the park is a sculpture known locally as 'Tonehenge', dedicated to the leader of the United Irishmen, Wolfe Tone (p222), while behind it is a memorial to the Irish Famine. There's also a statue of Countess Markiewicz, who led Republican insurgents against British government forces on the green during the Easter Rising of 1916.

Newman House

85-6 St Stephen's Green, **T** 01 716 7422. *Jun-Aug, Tue-Fri 1200, 1400, 1600. Closed Sep-May. €4. Bus 10, 11, 13B, 20B, 27C, 46A/B, 84X, 127, 129, 746. Map 2, E7, p249*

On the south side of St Stephen's Green are two Georgian houses, still undergoing renovation. Number 85 was designed by one of the city's greatest Georgian architects, Richard Castle, and later purchased by Richard (Burnchapel) Whaley, who had number 86 built along even grander lines. In 1865 the two houses were bought by the Catholic University of Ireland under the direction of John Henry Newman, and became its major lecture and accommodation centre. The poet Gerard Manley Hopkins lived

! On the north side of St Stephen's Green is the prestigious Shelbourne Hotel, which once employed Alois Hitler (half-brother of Adolf) as a wine waiter. Alois settled in Dublin, married and was later tried for bigamy here.

and taught at Newman House, and James Joyce, Padraig Pearse and Eamon de Valera all studied here. The guided tour takes in the ongoing renovations, plus Hopkins' room, and reveals the alterations made by the Jesuit university authorities in an effort to protect their innocent students from the immorality of the plaster nudes that decorated the ceilings. Next door is the 1855 Catholic University Church, which opens out, Tardis-fashion, from a tiny front entrance to reveal a majestic, colourful Byzantine interior.

● *Behind Newman House and accessed via Harcourt Street are the Iveagh Gardens. This secret park was formerly known as the Winter Gardens and was used in a 2001 TV film to represent St Stephen's Green during the 1916 Easter Rising. The gardens make a tranquil picnic spot, with a pretty waterfall, extensive lawns and a maze.*

Village quarter

Camden St, Wexford St and Aungier St.   *Bus 15, 16, 19.*
Map 2, D6-G6, p248

This typical working-class district of the city has some interesting streets and a good deal of history to explore. What's more, if you visit the village quarter at night, you'll discover that this is the place where young Dubliners, as opposed to young visitors, come to unwind. The **Bleeding Horse** pub (p149) on the corner of Charlotte Way dates back to the 17th century when troops from the battle of Rathmines brought their wounded animals here to be treated. Other pubs along this stretch that are worthy of note include **Cassidy's**, 42 Camden Street, which played host to Bill Clinton when he first visited Dublin, and **Whelan's** (p167), an excellent music venue. A tavern has stood on this spot for at least two centuries. Tucked between a bike shop and a bookie's, is a plaque marking the house where Robert Tressel, the author of the *Ragged Trousered Philanthropists*, was born in 1870. Tim Kelly, one of the Phoenix Park assassins of 1882 (p81), lived at 12 Wexford Street, before being hanged, aged 19, for his part in the plot. The junction of Wexford Street and Bishop Street is the location of the **Jacob's Biscuit Factory**, one of the most important battle sites during the 1916 Easter uprising, when a small group of rebels prevented British troops from reaching the city centre. In Aungier Street is **Whitefriar Street Carmelite Church** where the bones of St Valentine are supposedly kept.

Temple Bar and around

*Bordered by Dame Street to the south and the river Liffey to the north, **Temple Bar** takes its name from Sir William Temple, who in the 17th century had the bright idea of draining the wide marshy river banks that sloped down to the Liffey. In the years that followed, Temple Bar became the commercial heart of the city: boats brought goods into the district's warehouses, from where a network of roads carried them across the country. However, when the Custom House was built downriver in the late 18th century, the docks and warehouses followed and Temple Bar declined.*

Until the 1980s Temple Bar remained a run-down area of the city, waiting to be demolished for a new bus station. Now, this regenerated district is the pulsing heart of tourist Dublin. The smell of river mud mingles in the air with radicchio salad, expensive olive oil, Guinness and boxty, while the cobbled streets and designer alleyways are alive with the sounds of raucous, drunken laughter and Irish music.

*Temple Bar is a fun place to be, especially at night and in the summer when food, drink, music and crowds of people all combine to create a lively street vibe. Second-hand clothes shops, nifty galleries (the **Gallery of Photography** and the **National Photographic Archive** are the most notable), a glut of restaurants to suit most budgets, plenty of stylish coffeeshops and some popular nightclubs all add up to a real tourist treat. Temple Bar has very little to do with the Ireland of tradition that many visitors seek, but it's perfect if you're short on time and love waking up late in the morning, a bit hazy on the details but sure you had a great time.*

The most significant sights are located on the edge of Temple Bar, beyond the warren of little streets, but they're close enough and interesting enough to keep you in the area for a day at least. Wander into Temple Bar for lunch and out again to visit **Christchurch Cathedral** *or* **Dublin Castle**.

▶▶ *See Sleeping p109, Eating and drinking p133, Bars and clubs p153*

◉ Sights

Meeting House Square
Temple Bar. *Bus 77, 77A, 56A, 49, 125. Map 3, D5, p250*

One of the more successful developments in Temple Bar, this is an attractive modern space where a market is held on Saturdays (p189) and films are screened outdoors in summer (p161). Here you'll find the **Gallery of Photography** (*T 01 671 4654, Tue-Sat 1000-1800, Sun 1400-1800, free*), a purpose-built and carefully lit venue that displays a permanent collection of 20th-century Irish photographs, plus changing monthly exhibitions by Irish and international artists. Close by is the **National Photographic Archive** (*T 01 671 0073, Mon-Sat 1100-1800, Sun 1400-1800, free*), a collection of 300,000 photographs from the archive of the National Library of Ireland. The exhibitions cover the late 19th and early 20th centuries and reveal much about Dublin at the turn of the last century. Works by modern Irish photographers are also displayed.

● *Linking Temple Bar with the north side of the river is the newly refurbished, cast-iron Ha'penny Bridge. Erected in 1816, this the oldest remaining pedestrian river crossing in Dublin and an enduring symbol of the city. It was originally called Wellington Bridge but quickly acquired its current name due to the halfpenny toll that was levied on all users until 1919.*

Temple Bar
Follow the crowds to the heart of the city's most vibrant district.

★ Galleries

Best

- National Gallery of Ireland, p38
- Gallery of Photography, p47
- National Photographic Archive, p47
- Irish Museum of Modern Art, p54
- Dublin City Gallery, p69

Dublin Castle

Dame St, **T** 01 677 7129, www.dublincastle.ie *Guided tours Mon-Fri 1000-1700, Sat, Sun and public holidays 1400-1700. Closed Good Friday, Christmas. €4.50. Bus 77, 77A, 56A, 49 (from Eden Quay), 125 (from O'Connell St). Map 3, F3, p250*

Originally built in1204 by King John as a fortification to keep out the marauding native Irish, the castle you tour today is largely an 18th-century construct with 20th-century additions. The bulk of the guided tour is taken up with the State Apartments, which are still used for grand civic occasions; crystal chandeliers and plush Irish carpets endow the rooms with an incongruous posh-hotel feel. Check out the garish ceiling paintings in St Patrick's Hall. Among artefacts on display is an inlaid table created by some poor convict for Queen Victoria, only for her to leave it behind, not caring for the risqué design. You'll also visit the room where the wounded James Connolly was held captive, tied to a chair, after the Easter Rising in 1916. Through one of the windows you may glimpse a helicopter pad that covers the 'Black Pool' (*dubh linn* in Gaelic) from which the city takes its name. The tour concludes in the basement, where the remains of a Viking fortress have been partly excavated. After the tour, visit the castle's Chapel Royal, built in the 18th century by Francis Johnston, who was also responsible for the GPO building in O'Connell Street (p66).

● *On your way to the Viking undercroft, check out the suspect statue of Justice over the entrance gate: not only is she not wearing the traditional blindfold, but she has her back to the city that she should be protecting. What's more, until the statue was refurbished in the 1980s, the scales had a tendency to fill with water and tip over to one side whenever it rained.*

Chester Beatty Library

Dublin Castle, **T** 01 407 0750, www.cbl.ie *May-Sep Mon-Fri 1000-1700, Sat 1100-1700, Sun 1300-1700, Oct-Apr closed Mon. Closed public holidays. Free. Free tours Wed 1300, 1500, 1600. Bus 50, 50A, 54A (from Burgh Quay), 56A, 77, 77A, 77B (from Aston Quay).* Map 3, F4, p250

After festering away for years in the suburbs, the Chester Beatty Library is now housed in a beautifully converted old clock tower building within the castle walls. This priceless collection of cultural and religious treasures from all over the world was put together by Chester Beatty, a New York mining magnate of Irish descent, who bequeathed the collection to the Irish state on his death. It includes icons, early printed books, papyrus texts, over 250 copies of the Koran, ancient Bibles and Buddhas. One of the most beautiful items is a 10th-century fragment of a Kufic script, written in gold on blue vellum. The items on display are only a small portion of the complete collection.

City Hall

Cork Hill, Dame St, **T** 01 672 2204, www.dublincity.ie/cityhall *Mon-Sat 1000-1715, Sun and public holidays 1400-1700. Closed 24, 25 Dec. €4. Bus 50, 50A, 54A, 56A, 77, 77A, 77B.* Map 3, E3/4, p250

City Hall was built between 1769 and 1779 by Thomas Cooley as the city's Royal Exchange. Like much of the rest of Dublin, it fell into disuse after the Act of Union in 1800 and was taken over as an

Dublin's Coat of Arms

Dublin's Coat of Arms dates back to the 13th century and is seen all over the city, on benches and lamp posts, and in mosaic form on the floor of the Rotunda in City Hall. Great 'flames of zeal' gush from three fortified towers, framed by the female figures of Law on the left and Justice on the right. Flowers symbolize hope and happiness, and the quietistic Latin motto reads 'Happy the city where the citizens obey'.

administrative centre by the city corporation. The basement is now home to the 'Story of the Capital', a multi-media exhibition on the history of Dublin's civic government. It's a good warts-and-all introduction to the city, with displays ranging from a medieval 'Yellow Pages' to details of the protests against the construction of the Civic Offices on Wood Quay in 1978, which destroyed the most important Viking site in Ireland.

● *Before descending the stairs to the Story of the Capital exhibition, spend some time admiring the magnificent Rotunda ceiling and mosaic floor in the entrance hall.*

★ Christchurch Cathedral

Christchurch Place, **T** 01 679 8991, www.cccdub.ie *Mon-Fri 0945-1700, Sat and Sun 1000-1700. Treasures of Christchurch Mon-Fri 0945-1700, Sat 1000-1645, Sun 1230-1515. Bus 49, 50, 51B, 54A, 56A, 65, 77, 77A, 78A, 123. Exhibition €3. Donations €3.   Map 3, F1, p250*

This is Dublin's oldest building, pre-dating Dublin Castle by a century or so. The original wooden building of 1038 is long gone, and although the crypt, north wall and south transept date from the 12th century, the bulk of what you see is 19th-century stone cladding. It's a pretty but shabby kind of place, with lovely faux ancient floor tiles, a 16th-century replica of the tomb of Strongbow

(Richard de Clare, the Norman conqueror of Ireland) and lots of stuff to admire in the 'Treasures of Christchurch' exhibition in the crypt, from unwanted statues of the English kings Charles I and II to gold and silver church ornaments, ancient manuscripts and more. Stand in the choir by the bishop's throne and look back towards the entrance, and you'll notice that the north wall (to your right) is seriously out of kilter with the rest of the building.

Dublinia

St Michael's Hill, Christchurch, T 01 679 4611, www.dublinia.ie
Apr-Sep, Mon-Sun 1000-1700, Oct-Mar Mon-Sat 1100-1630. €5.75.
Bus 50 (from Eden Quay), 78A (from Aston Quay).   Map 2, B4, p248

Recently revamped, this is a presentation in sights and sounds of what life in medieval Dublin might have been like. Visitors can wander through a merchant's house, explore the kind of wooden ship that once docked at Wood Quay and play about with lots of hands-on gadgets. The best bit is a model of medieval Dublin that clearly shows how the ancient buildings and pathways still form the framework of the modern city. After the main exhibition, climb to the top of St Michael's Tower for a bird's-eye view of the city; the windows are rather grubby, but the skyline is explained for you.

The Liberties and west

In the early days of Dublin's development the network of streets known as the Liberties lay outside the city walls and formed one of many Gaelic self-governing districts. The 17th century saw it develop into a centre for the cloth industry, thanks to an influx of Huguenot refugees, many of whom were silk and linen weavers. Throughout the 20th century the Liberties remained a relatively run-down area of the city. It was designated as a digital media district in the 1990s, but expectations were inflated and the area's original working-class identity remains intact today.

The Liberties are home to the high-profile **Guinness Storehouse**, while further west are the **Irish Museum of Modern Art**, set in a beautiful old hospital building, and **Kilmainham Gaol**, lovingly restored after years of decay. Closer to town, at the southern end of the district, are **St Patrick's Cathedral** and **Marsh's Library**.

▸▸ *See Sleeping p111, Eating and drinking p137, Bars and clubs p155*

 Sights

★ Guinness Storehouse

St James's Gate, **T** 01 408 4800, www.guinness-storehouse.com *Daily 0930-1700. Closed 1 Jan, Good Friday and 24-26 Dec. €13.50. Bus 51B, 78A (from Aston Quay), 123 (from O'Connell St). Map 6, H12, p255*

One of the most popular and heavily marketed sights in Dublin, this stunningly converted brewery building is where advertising meets history. The Guinness brewery's 900-year lease of the St James's Gate site is embedded in the floor of a grand atrium shaped like a pint glass, while at the top of the building a circular bar offers 360-degree views of Dublin and a 'free' glass of Guinness to every adult visitor. There are loads of old Guinness adverts to enjoy here and assorted paraphernalia associated with the brewing process, but little that serves to highlight the non-Irish conglomerate that now owns the Guinness drink and brand.

Irish Museum of Modern Art

Royal Hospital, Military Rd, Kilmainham, **T** 01 612 9900, www.modernart.ie *Tue-Sat 1000-1730, Sun and bank holidays 1200-1730. Closed Mon, Good Friday, 24-26 Dec. Free. Guided tours May-Sep. €2. Bus 26 (from Wellington Quay), 51, 79 (from Aston Quay), 90 (from Connolly Station). Map 6, H8, p255*

The Royal Hospital at Kilmainham, which now houses the Irish Museum of Modern Art, was built between 1680 and 1684 as a retirement home for old soldiers. It was the first great classical structure to be built in Ireland, and its four great buildings around a central courtyard are well worth seeing for their architecture alone. The museum shows regularly changing exhibitions that combine pieces from its own collection with the work of guest artists. If you visit on a Thursday you can meet local and visiting artists at work in one of the studios.

After you have looked at the art, check out the programme of talks that take place here on a regular basis, or explore the formal 17th-century garden. There are pleasant walks from here across the meadow to **Bully's Acre**, a graveyard dating back at least a thousand years, where both the son and grandson of Brian Ború are said to have been buried after the Battle of Clontarf in 1014.

In summer there are guided tours of the hospital chapel, taking in the stunning original plasterwork, stained glass and woodcarvings, and of the Great Hall, which once served as the hospital dining room. Since 1731 it has been lined with portraits of assorted British bigwigs. These parts of the hospital complex are otherwise closed to visitors; check in advance for the exact times of tours.

★ Kilmainham Gaol
Inchicore Rd, **T** 01 453 5984, www.heritageireland.ie *Apr-Sep 0930-1700 daily, Oct-Mar Mon-Sat 0930-1600, Sun 1000-1700. Tour €5. Bus 51B, 78A, 79 (from Aston Quay). Map 6, I5, p254*

Pass through the gateway of the Gothic Richmond Tower and continue past the Patriot Inn (established in 1793) to reach Kilmainham Gaol, Ireland's most infamous prison. It opened in 1796 – just in time to incarcerate Wolfe Tone's rebel supporters in 1798 – and remained in service until 1924 when it was closed by the fledgling Republic. The gaol stood abandoned for 40 years until some history buffs began to do it up, and now it is a major tourist destination. Beyond the exhibition, which details the lives of some of the prison inmates, a guided tour takes you around the dungeons, past the tiny cells once occupied by such famous names in the struggle for Irish independence as Constance Markiewicz, Eamon de Valera and Padraig Pearse. You'll also see the chapel where Joseph Plunkett was married three hours before his execution, and the grim yard where James Connolly, Plunkett, and 15 other leaders of the 1916 uprising were executed.

St Patrick's Cathedral

Patrick's Close, **T** 01 475 4871, www.stpatrickscathedral.ie *Mar-Oct daily 0900-1800, Nov-Feb Mon-Fri 0900-1800, Sat 0900-1700, Sun 0900-1500. Closed 24-26 Dec, 1 Jan. €4. Bus 49X, 50, 50X, 54A, 56A, 77X. Map 2, D4, p248*

If Christchurch is the physical expression of the power of the Norman rulers of Ireland, St Patrick's is the people's cathedral. It supposedly stands on the site of a church founded by St Patrick himself, which makes it a considerably older Christian site than Christchurch – if the stories are true. The original stone building was constructed in 1192, only a few years after its rival, and, like Christchurch, St Patrick's was remodelled in the 19th century, with funding from one of the Guinness clan.

Despite its ugly Victorian exterior, St Patrick's is the more interesting of the two cathedrals, with much more of its medieval interior remaining intact. As you enter, look at the steps leading down to the main door, which indicate just how far the street level has risen in a thousand years. Inside is a ghastly, over-the-top wooden monument to the Boyle family and the door that,

> ! Both Christchurch and St Patrick's are Church of Ireland
> • (Anglican) Cathedrals, despite the fact that only 3% of Irish
> people are practising Anglicans.

apparently, gave us the expression 'chancing your arm'. In the 15th century the earls of Ormonde and Kildare began a fight in the church, only declaring a truce after a hole was cut in the door behind which Ormonde was hiding, thus allowing the two men to shake hands. The Lady Chapel at the east end of the church dates from the 13th century, and was used by the local Huguenot community during the 17th and 18th centuries.

Among many grandiose monuments to dead, rich folk, the cathedral also houses more noteworthy memorials to the satirist Jonathan Swift, who was Dean of St Patrick's during the 18th century, and to Turlogh O'Carolan, a poor and powerless composer and harpist. In the park outside the cathedral is St Patrick's well, which was used – so the story goes – by Paddy to baptize the local heathen population.

● *Jonathan Swift's epitaph is inscribed over the door of the cathedral robing room and reads: 'He lies where furious indignation can no longer rend his heart.'*

Marsh's Library
St Patrick's Close, **T** 01 454 3511, www.marshlibrary.ie *Mon 1000-1300, Wed-Fri 1000-1300, 1400-1700, Sat 1030-1300. Closed Tue and Sun. €2.50. Bus 50, 54A, 56A (from Eden Quay). Map 2, D4, p248*

A brief stroll along St Patrick's Close will take you from the cathedral to a Victorian iron gateway, which marks the entrance to Marsh's Library. Purpose built in 1701, this was Ireland's first public library and its interior has changed little since the 18th century. The still-functioning library now also operates as a small museum, with the signatures of famous readers, including James Joyce, on display alongside rare and ancient texts and some books annotated by Jonathan Swift. Check out the original library cages that were used to stop light-fingered readers from pilfering the books.

St Audoen's Church

Cornmarket, High St, **T** 01 677 0088, staudoenschurch@ealga.ie
Jun-Sep 0930-1730. Closed Oct-May. €2. Bus 123, 51B, 78A, 121.
Map 2, B3, p248

Dublin's oldest still-functioning parish church has much of its medieval interior intact. Admission includes access to a heritage centre, which describes the history of St Audoen's and the local guilds, and a tour of the church itself. Beside the church is a pretty little park and St Audoen's Gate, part of the medieval city walls.

Ballsbridge and south

*A short distance south of the city centre and with good bus routes for those unable or unwilling to walk, Ballsbridge is an expensive residential neighbourhood, whose postcode (Dublin 4) is synonymous with plummy accents, faux Victorian conservatories and undimmed middle-class values. To the north the **Grand Canal** separates Ballsbridge from the less salubrious but up-and-coming old Jewish quarter, where you can visit the **Irish Jewish Museum** and the house where **George Bernard Shaw** once lived.*
▸▸ *See Sleeping p111, Eating and drinking p138*

 Sights

Grand Canal

From Baggot St to Richmond St South. *Bus 5, 7, 7A, 10.*
Map 2, F12-H6, p248-9

A walk along the Grand Canal is possible if you don't mind the litter and the traffic, starting around Baggot Street where it crosses the canal and continuing as far as the Portobello district and beyond. If you're especially keen, the walkway actually follows the canal for over 100 km all the way to the river Shannon. En route from Baggot Street you'll pass a statue of Patrick Kavanagh ('the bench with the stench' as Dublin wit has it). The poet (1904-67) enjoyed sitting on the banks of the canal here, and the Kavanagh Seat is true to his express wishes: "O commemorate me with no hero courageous tomb, just a canal bank seat for the passers-by."

Irish Jewish Museum

3-4 Walworth St, off Victoria St. **T** 01 453 1797. *May-Sep Tue, Thu and Sun 1100-1530, Oct-Apr Sun only 1030-1430. Free. Bus 16, 16A, 19, 10A, 22, 22A. Map 2, H5, p248*

The Portobello area of Dublin, bordering the Grand Canal, was home to a thriving Jewish community from 1880 onwards. One of the synagogues has been restored as a museum of Jewish life in Ireland, with the place of worship faithfully recreated on the first floor and a reconstruction of a Jewish kitchen below. The exhibits tell the story of the dispiriting indifference shown by the Irish government to the plight of the Jews in Europe during the 1930s and '40s. Look out for the anti-semitic Sinn Féin poster from this period, and the letter from the Irish Chief Rabbi to President De Valera asking for visas for six Jewish medics. The request was turned down; in fact not a single Jewish refugee was admitted to Ireland during those years.

Shaw's Birthplace

33 Synge St, **T** 01 475 0854, www.visitdublin.com *May-Sept Mon-Sat 1000-1700, Sun and public holidays 1400-1800. €6. Bus 16, 19, 122. Map 2, F5, p248*

'Author of Many Plays' reads the plaque outside the house at 33 Synge Street where George Bernard Shaw was born, more or less summing up most people's perception of the playwright. Whether you're a fan of his work or not, the house itself is worth a visit for the quality of its Victorian interiors.

Crossing the great divide
The iconic Ha'penny Bridge forms a important link between the north and south sides of the city.

O'Connell Street and around

*Most of Dublin's much-touted visitor sights are located south of the river, but **O'Connell Street** on the north side has the genuine earthy feel of a working city to recommend it (not to mention fewer tour groups). The area has strong literary and historical associations, and the surrounding streets boast some of the city's earliest Georgian buildings. Especially worth visiting are the **Dublin City Gallery** and the **Dublin Writers' Museum**, and for Joyce aficionados there is also the **James Joyce Centre**.*

▸▸ *See Sleeping p114, Eating and drinking p140, Bars and clubs p155*

 ## Sights

O'Connell Street

Bus 7, 7A (from Ballsbridge), 121 (from Francis St), 746 (from St Stephen's Green),10, 11, 13 (from Kildare St), 20, 20B (from Connolly Station) and other cross-city buses. Map 5, F7/G7/H7, p253

A broad boulevard stretching half a kilometre north from the river to Parnell Square, O'Connell Street is dominated at each end by large nationalist monuments: Daniel O'Connell presides over the bottom of the street by the river, and Charles Stewart Parnell watches over the top. Both sides of the street are flanked by some grand early 20th-century buildings, constructed to replace the original 18th- and 19th-century ones that were destroyed by British artillery in 1916, while a tree-lined walkway stretches along the middle of the road, littered with more statuary. Look carefully at the O'Connell statue and you'll see the bullet marks that went astray during the attack on the GPO by British troops firing from the river. Other figures in stone include the radical nationalist leader, William Smith O'Connell; Father Theobald Matthew, founder of the Total Abstinence Movement, who seems rather

The day Lord Nelson lost his head

Nelson's Pillar on O'Connell Street was erected in 1808, long before the column on Trafalgar Square went up. Nelson stood on a hollow Doric column with an internal staircase that visitors could climb for a view over the city. This local landmark served as a bus and tram terminus until 1966, when, on the 50th anniversary of the Easter Rising, Sean Treacy, an IRA activist, stole a key to the pillar and planted explosives that rather neatly destroyed Nelson, but left most of the column standing. Pieces of Nelson, or rather pieces that people claimed to be part of Nelson, quickly went on sale, the head finding its way eventually to the Dublin Civic Museum, where it can be seen to this day. Later, explosives experts came in to demolish the column, causing considerably more damage to surrounding businesses than Treacy had done.

The destruction of Nelson's Pillar followed a long tradition of detonating imperial statuary in Dublin. William III was blown off his pediment in College Green in 1928 before being melted down and used to patch sewer pipes, George III and his horse copped it in the 1940s, as did the unfortunate George I, while Queen Victoria, who stood outside Leinster House was dismantled for safe keeping and found asylum in Australia.

For some reason no one has attacked the statue of Prince Albert that still stands outside the Natural History Museum, or, for that matter, the vast Wellington Memorial in Phoenix Park, although the statue of Viscount Hugh Gough, who fought with Wellington at Waterloo, had its head, legs and arms cut off, before being thrown into the Liffey and then blown up altogether.

More recently, the statue of Wolfe Tone on St Stephen's Green was hit in 1989 by the Ulster Volunteer Force, who presumably objected to the fact that Tone had aligned himself with the cause of Irish independence.

General Post Office
So much more than a place to buy stamps, the GPO served as the rebel headquarters during the 1916 Easter Rising.

out of place in the booze-filled street around midnight; Sir John Grey, who put in Dublin's drains and water supply; and James Larkin, a trade union leader who led resistance to the infamous Dublin lock-out by employers in 1913. Just off O'Connell Street in Earl Street is a statue of a dishevelled-looking James Joyce.

For over 150 years the space outside the General Post Office was occupied by a monumental pillar topped by a statue of Lord Nelson, till it was blown up by the IRA in1966 (p63). Nelson's Pillar was replaced by a statue of Anna Livia, the depressed-looking spirit of the river Liffey, fondly known by one and all as 'the whore in the sewer' (you have to hear a working-class Dubliner say it to hear the rhyme). She's now in storage and her prime site on O'Connell Street has been taken over by the towering Monument of Light (aka the 'stiletto in the ghetto'). Tapering from 3 m in diameter at its base to a mere 10 cm in the sky, the Monument of Light is lit internally at the very top, and by projections of light from surrounding buildings for most of its height of 120 m. The final piece was finally lifted into place in January 2003 and now passers-by comment on the likelihood of the monument blowing down and killing someone.

General Post Office

O'Connell St, **T** 01 705 7000. *Mon-Sat 0800-2000, Sun 1030-1830 (stamps only). All buses to O'Connell St. Map 5, G7, p253*

At the heart of the street, the GPO is much more than just the place to get your stamps. It was at the post office, rather than the City Hall or some other state building, that the rebels chose to make their stand against British forces during the 1916 Easter Rising, and where they made their declaration of independence. By the time

> **!**
> **•** A character in one of Samuel Beckett's novels attempts to commit suicide by repeatedly hitting his head against the GPO statue of Cúchulain.

> ### Monto
>
> For many years, the area east of O'Connell Street, known as Monto, was Dublin's red-light district, until civic authorities decided that such immoral goings-on did not sit well with the increasing importance of the Pro Cathedral. In 1925 all the resources of the Dublin police force were directed at a major clean-up of the area, in which every brothel that could be identified was officially closed down.
>
> This was followed by a sanctimonious procession of Catholic girls, who marched through the streets of Monto, attaching a holy picture to the erstwhile brothel doors.

the rebels surrendered, many of their number were dead, and the GPO was largely destroyed; only the façade of the original 1814 building survives today. Outside, check out the bullet marks on the columns of the portico, and inside admire a series of paintings depicting events of the battle. In a window stands a statue of Cúchulain, the mythical Irish hero whose determination and resistance has come to represent the heroic bravery of those who fought at the GPO in 1916.

Pro Cathedral

Marlborough St, **T** 01 874 5441, procath@dublindiocese.ie *Daily 0800-1830. Mass Mon-Sat 0830, 1000, 1100, 1245, 1745, Sun 1000, 1100, 1230, 1830. Bus 3 (from Pearse St DART), 10, 11 (from St Stephen's Green) and all buses to O'Connell St. Map 5, F7, p253*

Known as 'the Pro', this cathedral was built between 1815 and 1826 as part of the Catholic church-building spree that followed the relaxation of the Penal Laws, which had forbidden the practice of Catholicism. During the planning stages, Archbishop Troy had wanted the centre of Catholic worship in Ireland to be built on the

O'Connell Street site that was to become the GPO, but in the event a more discreet location was decided upon, so as not to offend the city's Protestant rulers. Built in the classical Greek style with Doric pillars and a central dome, the interior is notable for its simplicity of form and workaday functionality rather than any awe-inspiring atmosphere. The exterior portico is a later addition in keeping with the classical plainness of the original. The crypt, which contains the earthly remains of about 1,000 people, runs under Marlborough Road as far as the impressive Department of Education building, designed in the 1740s by Richard Castle.

Parnell Square
Top of O'Connell St. *All buses to O'Connell St.* Map 5, E6/F6, p252

At the north end of O'Connell Street, the statue of Parnell looms over the buildings of the **Rotunda Hospital** on the southern edge of Parnell Square. In 1748 the undeveloped land here was laid out as a pleasure garden by the barber-surgeon Dr Bartholomew Mosse and the Georgian gentry came in their horses and carriages to pay for the enjoyment of a stroll in the best area of the city. The profits from Mosse's pleasure garden funded the construction of a free maternity hospital officially named the Dublin Lying-In Hospital, but universally known as the Rotunda. Mosse and his successors later built the Rotunda Room and the Assembly Rooms (part of which now form the Gate Theatre, p171) as social venues to raise money to cover the hospital's costs.

A stately city square gradually developed around the gardens, with each house separately commissioned by some local aristo, including Lord Wicklow (No 4) and the Earl of Ormonde (No 11). Number five was later inhabited by Oliver St John Gogarty, best known for being lampooned by James Joyce in *Ulysses* as Buck Mulligan. Most of the north part of the square is taken up by a grand house that was built for Lord Charlemont (owner of the Casino at Marino, p84) and now contains the Dublin City Gallery.

At the centre of the square is the **Garden of Remembrance**, created in 1966 to commemorate the deaths of the Irish volunteers in the 1916 uprising. When they surrendered at the GPO, those who survived were marched to this spot and held in the gardens overnight before being taken to Kilmainham Gaol (p55). A commemorative statue, *The Children of Lir*, by Oisin Kelly was added in 1971.

According to Irish legend, Lir was the god of the sea whose three children were turned into swans by their stepmother and doomed to swim the shores of Ireland for 900 years. When they finally staggered ashore as humans once more, they died of old age. In front of the statue, a pool full of broken spears represents the ancient custom of throwing weapons into a lake or river as an offering to the gods when a battle is over.

● *Visit the chapel on the first floor of the Rotunda Hospital, above the main entrance, to admire the amazing stucco work showing Faith blindfolded with Bible and cross, Hope holding an anchor and Charity feeding an infant. There is also a herd of cherubim and archangel Gabriel blowing a trumpet. The dull coats of arms represent the distinguished Dublin nobs who coughed up money for the hospital. Mass is held here at 0900 on Sundays.*

Dublin City Gallery 'Hugh Lane'

Charlemont House, Parnell Sq North, **T** 01 874 1903, www.hughlane.ie *Tue-Thu 0930-1800, Fri and Sat 0930-1700, Sun 1000-1700. Closed Mon. Permanent exhibition free. Francis Bacon Studio €7. Bus 3, 10, 11, 13, 16, 19. Map 5, E6, p252*

This grand 18th-century town house holds one of the most important collections of modern Irish and international art in the country, including works by Corot, Monet, Degas, Burne Jones and Manet, among many others. It also has the world's largest holding of work by 20th-century Irish painters such as Jack Yeats, Walter Osborne, Sarah Purser and Norman Garstin. In the entrance lobby

★ Georgian architecture

Best

- Merrion Square, p41
- Newman House, p44
- Henrietta Street, p71
- Mountjoy Square, p72
- Custom House, p73

look out for Seamus Murphy's heroically proportioned homage to Michael Collins in marble. The stained glass room contains *The Eve of St Agnes,* the best known work of the artist Harry Clarke, whose strange style borders on the surreal. You can see more of Clarke's work in the National Gallery (p38;*The Song of the Mad Prince*), and, strangely, in Bewley's Café on Grafton Street (p131).

Upstairs is the faithfully reconstructed studio of Francis Bacon, probably Ireland's greatest artist. Each of the 80,000 items from Bacon's London studio was picked up one at a time, brought to Ireland and replaced in exactly the same position in the gallery: empty beer bottles, dried-up paintbrushes, plastic bags and all.

Dublin Writers' Museum

18 Parnell Sq North, **T** 01 872 2077, www.visitdublin.com *Sep-May Mon-Sat 1000-1700, Sun and public holidays 1100-1700, Jun-Aug Mon-Fri 1000-1800, Sat 1000-1700, Sun and public holidays 1100-1700. €6. Bus 10, 11, 13, 13A, 16, 16A, 19. Map 5, E6, p252*

Two of the 18th-century houses in Parnell Square are now occupied by the Dublin Writers' Museum, which displays rare books and memorabilia associated with famous Irish writers including Swift, Sheridan, Wilde, Shaw, O'Casey, Yeats, Joyce, Beckett, Behan and Heaney. There are some decent paintings too, including Jacques-Emile Blanche's famous portrait of James Joyce. The buildings themselves are quite beautiful, with complex friezes surrounding the original Adam-esque ceilings. There's also a pleasant coffee shop on site, and a bookshop where you can buy the works of the museum's featured authors.

James Joyce Centre

35 North Great George St, **T** 01 878 8547, www.jamesjoyce.ie
Mon-Sat 0930-1700, Sun and public holidays 1200-1500. Closed 24-27 and 31 Dec, 1 Jan. €4.50. Bus 3, 10, 11, 11A, 13, 16, 16A, 19, 19A, 22, 22A. Map 5, E7, p253

Dedicated to the life and work of Ireland's most famous literary figure, the James Joyce Centre is unmissable for anyone with an interest in the writer. Most visits begin with an absorbing video of archive film about his life in early 20th-century Dublin. The building is filled with portraits and photographs of Joyce's family and people associated with his writing. Of particular note is the series of photographs taken in the 1950s, showing Dublin venues that are mentioned in Joyce's books, but no longer exist today. Upstairs in the library is an impressive collection of literature, plus tapes of Joyce reading from his works. As well as books, the shop sells videos of films based on Joyce's fiction, such as John Huston's memorable adaptation of *The Dead*. During the annual Bloomsday festival (9-17 June) lots of events are held at the centre (p176).

Georgian north Dublin

Henrietta St and Mountjoy Sq. *Bus to Parnell Square, then 5-min walk east or west.* Map 5, F4, p252 and D7/8, p253

Following the initial development of O'Connell Street and the surrounding Georgian terraces in the 18th century, north Dublin became the grandest and most salubrious area of the city. One street that has maintained its character from this time is **Henrietta Street**, a brief walk west from Parnell Square, which was created by the property magnate Luke Gardiner in 1730 and

The Boardwalk

The Liffey Boardwalk is a 4-m-wide walkway stretching alongside the river between O'Connell Bridge and Grattan (Capel Street) Bridge. It is designed to provide greater access to the Liffey along what was, until recently, a fairly run-down stretch of the north Dublin quays. When the extended walkway across Grattan Bridge is finally completed, the two sides of the river – Temple Bar with its boutique-style shops and Henry Street with its oddball stores – will be linked, creating a pedestrianized zone across the Liffey and helping to end the polarization of north and south Dublin that the river has always created.

named after his daughter. For almost a century Henrietta Street was the most desirable address in Dublin: in 1792 four peers, four MPs, two bishops and an archbishop lived there, alongside the Gardiner family, who resided at number 10 until 1854.

After the Act of Union, Dublin's rich and famous retired to their country seats and this area of the city fell into a sharp decline. The grand houses were bought up and divided into tenement buildings by avaricious entrepreneurs, with as many as 20 apartments in a single house, each occupied by a large, impoverished Irish family. Not surprisingly, disease spread like wild fire through the overcrowded, unheated and unsanitary buildings. As recently as 1975 there were 36 people living at 13 Henrietta Street, and it is only in the last decade or so that the area has begun to emerge from years of poverty and neglect.

East of Parnell Square, **Mountjoy Square** is an even better preserved relic of the grand days of Georgian north Dublin. Built between 1792 and 1818 by Lord Mountjoy, the grandson and namesake of Luke Gardiner, the square is formed from four solid edifices facing inwards on to a private garden. Like the rest of

Georgian Dublin, Mountjoy Square went through a period of decline and re-emergence, but has survived the experience remarkably intact, with most buildings faithfully restored to their former glory.

Ulysses fans will recognize the square as the place where Leopold Bloom bumps into David Sheehy, MP, a genuine resident of the square in 1904, when the novel is set. Sheehy was the father of the more famous Hannah Sheehy Skeffington, a feminist and suffragette, whose pacifist husband, Francis Skeffington, was killed during the 1916 Easter Rising.

The east side of Mountjoy Square is the most authentic façade, while the west and south sides have been more or less completely rebuilt in the original style. Sean O'Casey lived at number 35 and used it as the setting for his Dublin play *The Shadow of a Gunman*. Call into the wine merchants at number 25 to see part of an original Georgian interior.

Custom House

Custom House Quay, **T** 01 888 2538. *Mid Mar-Nov, Mon-Fri 1000-1230, Sat and Sun 1400-1700, Nov-mid Mar, Wed-Fri 1000-1230, Sun 1400-1700. €1. DART Tara St. Map 5, G9, p253*

Designed by the great James Gandon, and built between 1781 and 1791, the Custom House is constructed in neo-classical style, reminiscent of the architecture of ancient Rome. Inside the building are displays on the architecture of Dublin, the stormy history of the Custom House itself and anecdotes about the various people associated with it, such as the novelist Flann O'Brien, who worked as a civil servant here in the 1940s.

! The construction of the Custom House was bitterly opposed by merchants based further up river. Gandon had to carry a sword for protection, gangs were regularly sent to attack the builders, and in 1789 the place was set alight.

Grand designs
Gandon's Custom House dominates the cityscape north of the river.

Best

★ **View points**

- Guinness Storehouse, p54
- Chimney Viewing Tower, p78
- Dalkey, p94
- Bray Head, p95
- Howth Head, p98

After visiting the exhibition take a walk along Moss Street on the south side of the river to admire in full the building's beautiful exterior and marvellous skyline. The four figures standing above the pediment are Neptune and Mercury at each end, with Industry and Plenty between them. On top of the dome stands Commerce, surrounded by ornately carved pots that once concealed the building's chimneys. The Custom House's copper dome and the columnar drum on which it rests were completely destroyed when the IRA burned the building down in 1921, as one of the final acts of aggression in the Irish War of Independence. It is easy to see that the replacement limestone from County Meath has discoloured at a faster rate than the original Portland stone below it.

● *On Custom House Quay look out for the striking sculpture by Ronan Gillespie, which commemorates victims of the Great Famine.*

From Smithfield to the Phoenix Park

Originally the site of a run-down fruit and vegetable market and a horse fair, **Smithfield** *has in recent years become the centre of an ambitious urban redevelopment scheme, with riverside public housing, a flash hotel and a growing population of bars and restaurants surrounding a vast public space that is lit on Saturday nights by gigantic gas braziers. The horse fair has since vacated the new cobbled plaza and now takes place further up the road, but the fruit and vegetable market still struggles on, despite these*

*incongruous surroundings. Between here and the city centre is the
imposing **Four Courts** building, constructed by James Gandon in
1802, and ancient **St Michan's Church**. Further west lies **Collins
Barracks**, now an entertaining part of the National Museum, and
the **Phoenix Park**, where you'll find newly refurbished **Dublin Zoo**,
the home of the Irish President and an ancient tower house.*

▸▸ *See Sleeping p118, Eating and drinking p144, Bars and clubs p157*

◉ Sights

★ National Museum of Decorative Arts and History
Collins Barracks, Benburb St, **T** 01 677 7444, www.museum.ie
*Tue- Sat 1000-1700, Sun 1400-1700. Free. Guided tours €1.50.
Bus 25, 66, 67, 90 (from Aston Quay).* Map 6, F11/12, p255

These beautiful buildings were, for a long time, the largest military
barracks in Europe, designed by Thomas Burgh in 1701 to house
5,000 men, and only finally decommissioned in 1969.

They now contain the National Museum's collection of decorative
arts, with a huge variety of exhibits laid out in innovative ways. The
favourite pieces of the museum's curator form one display, and
another room is full of objects grouped together for their aesthetic
value rather than to illustrate a piece of history. Drawers can be
opened to reveal exquisite accoutrements, while a fascinating
collection of rural furniture and crafts is accompanied by audio-visual
material on traditional skills that are on the verge of dying out. This
exhibit provides a vivid contrast to displays of lavish costumes and
costly furniture owned by Ireland's upper classes.

On the top floor look out for the clock whose inner workings
have been lowered to eye level so that visitors can watch the
intricate whirrings. (Catch it on the hour when the clock chimes.)
Also on the top floor is an exhibition of the work of Eileen Gray
(1878-1976) , one of Ireland's most famous 20th-century designers.

Old Jameson Distillery

Bow St, Smithfield Village, **T** 01 807 2355. *Daily 0900-1800. Closed 25 Dec, Good Friday. Last tour at 1730. €7. Bus 67, 68, 69, 79, 90. Map 5, H2, p252*

Jameson is now owned by the Irish Distillery Company, which also owns the Power, Paddy and Bushmills brands, and most of its whiskey is produced at Middleton in County Cork. This Dublin site closed as a working distillery long ago, and the buildings are now a museum dedicated to the history of whiskey production. The guided tour starts with a short audio-visual show before visiting the grain store and continuing on through the malting, milling, mashing, distilling and bottling processes, taking in the old copper stills, fermentation vessels and all the other paraphernalia of whiskey manufacture.

There is a bar and a complimentary tipple at the end of the tour, but if you are keen to try more than one whiskey, then hurl yourself forward for the voluntary tasting session. This involves comparing the taste of four Irish whiskeys, a Scotch whisky and a Bourbon, before tottering away with a certificate to prove your connoisseurship. Additional drinks can be purchased at the distillery bar, including the very rare and expensive Middleton whiskey at €9.20 a shot.

Chimney Viewing Tower

Smithfield Village, **T** 01 817 3800, www.chiefoneills.com *Mon-Sat 1000-1730, Sun 1100-1730. €5. Bus 25, 67 (from Middle Abbey St) 68, 69, 79 (from Aston Quay), 90 (from Connolly, Tara St or Heuston Stations). Map 5, H2, p252*

The 185 ft (54 m) chimney of the former Jameson Distillery was built in 1895 and has now been converted into a viewing tower as part of the regeneration of Smithfield. A glass-walled lift takes you to the top from where you can gaze out over the city.

Four Courts
Administering law and order beside the Liffey.

St Michan's Church

Church St, **T** 01 872 4154, www.stmichans@iol.ie *Mar-Oct, Mon-Fri 1000-1230 and 1400-1630, Sat 1000-1245, Nov-Feb, Mon-Fri 1230-1530, Sat 1000-1245. €3.50. Bus 25, 25A, 26, 37, 51, 66, 66A, 68, 69, 134. Map 5, H3, p252*

St Michan's was founded in 1095 by Viking settlers. None of the original building survives, although the grey limestone tower dates from the 15th century. The rest of the church has been rebuilt many times, in the 17th and 19th centuries, and again in the 1920s following damage caused during the Civil War.

St Michan's chief claim to fame is the display of centuries-old corpses in its vaults, which have been preserved for years by the magnesium salts in the limestone. Among the bodies are the two Sheares brothers, who were executed for taking part in the 1798 rebellion and really deserve a better fate than becoming part of a ghoulish tourist attraction. Above ground is the organ on which Handel practised for the first performance of his *Messiah*.

Phoenix Park

Visitor Centre, **T** 01 677 0095, www.heritageireland.ie *Jan-Mar, daily 1000-1700, Apr-Sep, daily 1000-1800, Oct, daily 1000-1700, Nov and Dec, Sat and Sun 1000-1700. €2.75. Bus 37 (from Middle Abbey St). Map 6, p254*

It is easy to spend a whole day pottering between the sights of the Phoenix Park. This is the largest enclosed public park in Europe, and its 1,752 acres (710 ha) enclose Dublin Zoo, a police museum, a visitor centre, Ashtown Castle (a tiny 17th-century tower house), a Neolithic cromlech, the ruins of a magazine fort, monuments to assorted public figures (including a vast obelisk dedicated to Wellington and a cross marking a papal visit in 1979), the homes of both the Irish President (Áras an Uachtaráin) and the American ambassador, not to mention several lakes, ancient trees and herds of deer. Dubliners use the Phoenix Park for all sorts of activities from practising their golf swings to flying model aeroplanes, playing hurling matches or just sitting about in the sunshine.

There's not much to see in the **visitor centre** apart from stiff-looking waxwork figures, but admission includes a guided tour of **Ashtown Castle**. On Saturdays there are also hourly free tours of **Áras an Uachtaráin**. When you visit, look out for the plaque on the road outside, which marks the places where members of the Irish Republican Brotherhood assassinated Lord Cavendish, the Lord Lieutenant of Ireland, and his under-secretary in May 1882. If your legs get tired, a shuttle bus runs from the main gates to the visitor centre, stopping off at the zoo and the papal cross.

● *Built in 1735 the magazine fort in Phoenix Park seems to serve no useful purpose, nor ever did as this jingle by Jonathan Swift proclaims: "Behold!/ A proof of Irish sense;/ How Irish wit is seen!/ When nothing's left/ That's worth defence/ We build a magazine."*

Dublin Zoo
Phoenix Park, **T** 01 474 8900, www.dublinzoo.ie *Mar-Sept, Mon-Sat 0930-1800, Sun 1030-1800. Oct-Feb, Mon-Sat 0930-dusk, Sun 1030-dusk. Last admission 1 hr before closing. €10. Bus 10 (from O'Connell St), 25, 26 (from Wellington Quay). Train Heuston Station.* Map 6, B6, p254

Established in 1830, Dublin Zoo has recently been enlarged and is now very child friendly. It occupies 66 acres and includes a city farm, an enclosure called the African Plains, a discovery centre and a zoo train. Several endangered species are represented here.

Glasnevin and Clontarf

*Spreading north from the Royal Canal, which marks the edge of Dublin's city centre, are the twin suburbs of Glasnevin and Clontarf, largely residential areas characterized by some attractive Edwardian estates full of much sought-after terraced houses. Apart from the area's bed and breakfast accommodation, visitors are drawn here by two major attractions: the **National Botanic Gardens** and **Prospect Cemetery** at Glasnevin. These sights are close enough to each other to be visited on the same day. Slightly nearer to the centre is **Croke Park** stadium, the home of Gaelic games.*

▸▸ *See Sleeping p119*

 ## Sights

Prospect Cemetery

Finglas Rd, Glasnevin, **T** 01 830 1133, www.glasnevin-cemetery.ie
Daily dawn-dusk. Free. Guided tours from the main gate Oct-Apr, Wed and Fri 1430, May-Sep, extra tour Sun 1130. Bus 40, 40A, 40B, 40C.
Map 1, A3, p247

This is the final resting place for scores of the country's leading political, literary and cultural figures. Dominating the scene is the faux ancient tower vault that holds most of the earthly remains of Daniel O'Connell (they left his heart in the Vatican) plus lots of his male descendants. Until 1971 you could climb to the top of the tower, but a bomb in that year took out the stairs. Parnell is also buried in the cemetery, as is De Valera, whose grave has been periodically vandalized, presumably by those with bitter memories of the Civil War. Michael Collins is here, too, in a big, lonely-looking plot all to himself, with his fiancée Kitty Kiernan nearby. Seek out the grave of Gerard Manley Hopkins in the Jesuit plot and a whole village of past bishops taking up one corner of the graveyard. Close to

O'Connell's tower and De Valera's grave is the Republican plot, which has a particularly high concentration of famous bodies. Brendan Behan's grave has a carved hole that once held a statue of the writer. The cemetery guide may inform you that a pint of (empty?) Guinness is now sometimes found in its place.

The actual designs of the graves themselves are almost as interesting as the people who lie beneath them. Grand mausoleums mark the life and death of people with cash to spare, while more modest gravestones note the passing of the cemetery's other million and a quarter inhabitants. There are mass graves for the victims of the cholera epidemics that decimated the city's population and other blank spaces where famine victims were interred. Grave robbing was a common practice during the 19th century, which explains the guard towers along the perimeter of the cemetery. The enjoyable and informative free guided tours are recommended.

National Botanic Gardens

Finglas Rd, Glasnevin, **T** 01 857 0909, botanicsv@ealga.ie *Summer, Mon-Sat 0900-1800, Sun 1100-1630, winter, Mon-Sat 1000-1630, Sun 1100-1630. Access to the glasshouses and Alpine house may be more limited. Free. Guided tours €2 by prior arrangement. Bus 13, 19 (from O'Connell St), 134 (from Middle Abbey St). Map 1, A4, p247*

The National Botanic Gardens cover 500 acres and are planted with 20,000 species of indigenous and exotic plants. Established in 1795, they are worth a visit merely for the chance to admire the great 19th-century glasshouses. The Gardens are currently undergoing a massive, long-term facelift that has completely replaced the curvilinear greenhouses, and added a new Alpine house and a visitor centre with a good café. Elsewhere, check out the rock garden, arboretum, Burren area (based on the limestone geology of County Clare), plus displays of Victorian carpet bedding and plenty more.

GAA Museum

Croke Park, **T** 01 855 8176, www.gaa.ie *Mon-Sat 0930-1700, Sun 1200-1700. Open to Cusack Stand ticket holders only on match days. Closed Good Friday and Christmas. Museum €5, museum and tour €8.50. Bus 3, 11, 11A, 16, 16A, 123, 51A. Map 5, A10, p253*

Definitely one for sports fans, this museum explores the history of the Gaelic Athletic Association and the assorted Irish games played at Croke Park, including hurling, Gaelic football and camogie (a hurling-type game played by women). The tour takes you around the stadium and past Hill 16, named after the 16 spectators who were gunned down by British 'Black and Tans' in 1920 as a reprisal against the assassination of 11 British Intelligence officers by nationalists led by Michael Collins. For details of matches held at Croke Park, see p193.

Casino at Marino

Off Malahide Rd, Marino, **T** 01 833 1618, www.heritageireland.ie *Feb, Mar, Nov and Dec, Sat and Sun 1200-1600, Apr, Sat and Sun 1200-1700, May and Oct daily 1000-1700, Jun-Sep daily 1000-1800. €2.75. Bus 20A, 20B, 27, 27B, 42, 42C, 123 (from O'Connell St). DART Clontarf Rd. Map 1, A7, p247*

This 18th-century gentleman's residence was commissioned by the Earl of Charlemont and designed by Sir William Chambers. Work began in the late 1750s in the grounds of a country house that has long since disappeared. Although the Casino looks like a miniature Greek temple from the south, the building is in fact a three-storey house, with chimneys disguised as urns and Ionic columns serving as drainpipes. The casino was derelict by the 1930s, but it is now owned by the state and its 16 rooms are open to the public, by guided tour only. It is a whimsical place, full of secret staircases and clever architectural tricks.

North Bull Island Interpretive Centre

North Bull Island, **T** 01 833 8341. *Mon-Fri 1015-1300 and 1330-1530, Sat and Sun 1000-1300 and1330-1630. Free. Bus 130. Map 7, p256*

North Bull Island is relatively new territory, having been created since the building of the North Bull Wall in 1820 at the suggestion of Captain Bligh (of Mutiny on the Bounty fame). It is given over to the ubiquitous lumps and bumps of a golf course, but also happens to be the winter residence of thousands of migratory birds, as well as more common wildlife residents, who eke out an existence dodging golf balls and motor mowers. The interpretive centre identifies some of the species to be seen on the island.

It's possible to reach the island on foot along the river Liffey from Clontarf, taking in lots of little strips of parkland between the road and the water. All along the route you will have views across the river to the post-industrial landscapes and building sites along the south bank.

Dublin

Museums and galleries

Listings

- **Book of Kells Exhibition** The top attraction at Trinity College is a masterpiece of religious craftsmanship, p34.
- **Chester Beatty Library** A stunning collection of ancient manuscripts and artwork, p51.
- **City Hall** The former Royal Exchange houses the worthwhile Story of the Capital exhibition, p51.
- **Dalkey Castle** An ancient building with exhibits that trace the history of Dalkey. Great views, p94.
- **Douglas Hyde Gallery** A shifting collection of conceptual and avant-garde art fits well into this large bland area of the 1980s-built Paul Koralec Arts Block, p34.
- **Dublin Castle** Explore the State Apartments, the medieval remains in the undercroft and the Chapel Royal, p50.
- **Dublin City Gallery** (aka the Hugh Lane Gallery) Exciting collection of 19th- and 20th-century artworks, donated to the nation by Sir Hugh Lane. Highlights include the reconstruction of Francis Bacon's studio, p69.
- **Dublin Civic Museum** 58 South William St, T 01 679 4260, www.dublincitycouncil.ie *Tue-Sat 1000-1800, Sun 1100-1400. Closed bank holiday weekends.* Once the city's Assembly House, this historic building relates the history of the city, with old maps, street furniture and Nelson's head, p63.
- **Dublinia** An insight into life in medieval Dublin, p53.
- **Dublin Writers' Museum** Dedicated to Irish writers and their work, p70.
- **GAA Museum** History of Ireland's national sports, p84.
- **Gallery of Photography** First-rate temporary exhibitions as well as a permanent collection of contemporary photography by Irish artists. Good bookshop, p47.
- **Guinness Storehouse** A temple to the famous Irish drink and brand, p54

Museums and galleries

- **Heraldic Museum** 2 Kildare St, **T** 01 603 0311, www.nli.ie *Mon-Wed 1000-2000, Thu and Fri 1000-1630, Sat 1000-1230.* Exhibition of Irish heraldry.
- **Irish Jewish Museum** Museum commemorating the lives of the city's Jewish community, p59.
- **Irish Museum of Modern Art** Displays from the museum's permanent collection of modern conceptual art, plus exhibitions set in a beautiful 17th-century building, p54.
- **James Joyce Centre** The life and works of James Joyce, p71.
- **James Joyce Museum** A Martello tower houses literary memorabilia associated with Joyce and *Ulysses*, p93.
- **Malahide Castle** The home of the Talbot family has portraits and period furniture, while the extensive grounds contain the Fry Model Railway and a botanic garden, p99.
- **Marsh's Library** Ireland's first public library contains classical and liturgical texts, with scrawls by Jonathan Swift, p57.
- **National Gallery of Ireland** About 2,000 paintings and 10,000 other works are held by the gallery, representing most major European schools of art. The renowned collection of Irish paintings, includes a special selection of JB Yeats' work, p38.
- **National Maritime Museum** Boaty paraphenalia in Dun Laoghaire, p92.
- **National Museum of Archaeology and History** Artefacts dating from prehistoric Ireland through to the early years of the 20th century, including wonderful Bronze Age gold, p37.
- **National Museum of Decorative Arts and History** Ireland's social and economic progress is explored through beautiful decorative art exhibits, p77.
- **National Museum of Natural History** Victorian cabinets display an enormous collection of stuffed wildlife from Ireland and overseas, p39.

Listings

Dublin

Museums and galleries

Listings

- **National Photographic Archive** Some 300,000 photographs from the National Library of Ireland's collection, p47.
- **National Print Museum** Beggar's Bush, Haddington Rd, T 01 660 3770. *Mon- Fri 1000-1700, Sat, Sun and bank holidays 1200-1500.* A unique assortment of machinery connected with the early days of printing, from early typesetters to computers.
- **National Transport Museum** Sixty exhibits relating to the history of transport, p98.
- **Number 29** A beautifully restored Georgian residence, p41
- **Old Jameson Distillery** Learn all about whiskey manufacture and sample the finished product, p78.
- **Pearse Museum** St Enda's Park, Grange Rd, Rathfarnham, T 01 493 4208, www.heritageireland.ie *Feb-Apr and Sep-Oct, daily 1400-1700, Nov-Jan, daily 1400-1600, May-Aug, daily 1400-1730.* The former school run by Patrick Pearse is now a museum dedicated to his memory.
- **Rathfarnham Castle** Rathfarnham, Dublin 14, T 01 493 9462, www.heritageireland.ie *May-Oct, daily 0930-1730.* €2. This 16th-century castle has 18th-century interiors designed by Sir William Chambers. It's still undergoing renovation, but visitors will get a lot out of observing the restoration process.
- **RHA Gallagher Gallery** 15 Ely Place, T 01 661 2558. *Tue, Wed, Fri, Sat 1100-1700, Thu 1100-2000, Sun 1400-1700.* Large exhibition space dedicated to contemporary and modern art.
- **Shaw's Birthplace** More an insight into Victorian Dublin than the life and works of GB Shaw, p59.
- **Waterways Visitor Centre** Grand Canal Quay, T 01 677 7510, www.waterwaysireland.org *Jun-Sep, daily 0930-1830, Oct-May, Wed-Sun 1230-1700.* The 'Box in the Docks', as the locals like to call it, explores the history and ecology of Ireland's inland waterways and canals.

South of Dublin 91 One of the best things about Dublin is its proximity to some beautiful countryside and coastal towns. To the south of the city a host of seaside villages retain their charm despite rapidly being subsumed by the city's suburbs. Take the scenic DART as far as Dun Laoghaire to enjoy a bracing walk along the harbour wall, or visit the Joyce Tower, where the writer set the opening of *Ulysses*. Beyond are the exclusive villages of Dalkey and Killiney, and the resort of Bray, which has a grand Victorian seafront and access to some lovely walks.

North of Dublin 95 To the north of the city, Howth is a slightly run-down seaside town with great walks around Howth Head, while at Malahide there's a castle and gardens to explore. Beyond is Skerries, where you'll find thatched cottages, music pubs and sandy beaches. Further north again, in County Meath, is unmissable Newgrange, an amazing 5,000-year-old passage grave that predates Stonehenge and the Egyptian pyramids.

South of Dublin

*The DART runs right along the south coast of Dublin Bay as far as **Dun Laoghaire**, with its massive harbour and ferry port, and on to **Bray**, where you can enjoy the faded seaside atmosphere and a lovely cliff walk. In between, coastal villages offer a complete change of pace from the frenetic city centre. **Dalkey** and **Killiney** have become fashionable retreats for Ireland's rich and famous, but still retain enough character to be worth a visit, even if you're not interested in celeb-spotting. This whole area is very child-friendly, with sea trips, a touchy-feely marine attraction at Bray, and plenty of beaches and swimming spots to keep the whole family amused.*

▸▸ *See Sleeping p120, Eating and drinking p144*

 ## Sights

Towards Dun Laoghaire
DART Booterstown, Blackrock and Seapoint. Map 7, p256

Consider getting off the DART for a few minutes at **Booterstown** where the marsh, right beside the track, is home to some interesting birds that are identified on a panel on the station platform. The next stop is **Blackrock**, which once marked the furthest outskirts of the city, but is now a wealthy suburb of Dun Laoghaire. There is a good Sunday market here with craft and clothes stalls (p189) , two shopping centres and lots of pubs and cafés. Beside the DART station, Blackrock Park looks out over the sea, and at 1 Main Street, next to the shops, is an ancient cross carved with the effigy of a human face, possibly early Christian in origin. There is a pleasant walk along the seafront from here, following the DART all the way to Dun Laoghaire. On the way, look out for an excellent swimming beach near the old **Seapoint** open-air baths.

Dun Laoghaire
DART Dun Laoghaire. Map 7, p256

Originally a fishing village on Dublin Bay, Dun Laoghaire (pronounced 'Dun Leary') became a major resort and harbour following the completion of its two mile-long piers in 1827, and was renamed Kingstown in honour of George IV, who visited in 1820. (It didn't get its original name back until 1922.) In the mid century, Dun Laoghaire became an important safe haven for the British fleet, and took over from Howth (p96) as the destination for mail and packet ships. Yacht owners were also attracted by the harbour, founding the Royal Yacht Club in 1850. The arrival of the railway brought day-trippers from the city and further afield, and hotels and boarding houses were built to accommodate them.

Since the 1960s, Dun Laoghaire has been familiar to most visitors as the port for car ferries crossing the Irish Sea. Stena Line's high-speed ferry (p24) regularly swishes in and out of the harbour, with warning signs telling pedestrians to keep away while the boat is docking or departing. Apart from its role as a port, however, Dun Laoghaire has several claims on your time and offers a break from the traffic and fuss of the city. Walk out along the harbour's **east pier** to enjoy panoramic views of Dublin Bay and occasional concerts in the bandstand, or stroll along the grand seafront, backed by disapproving Victorian houses, en route towards Sandycove, Dalkey, Killiney and Bray.

National Maritime Museum
Mariner's Church, Haigh Terrace, Dun Laoghaire, **T** 01 280 0969. *May-Sep, daily 1300-1700. €2. DART Dun Laoghaire. Bus 46B, €2. Map 7, p256*

One of those cranky little museums filled with oddball stuff, this place is home to a ship's longboat captured during the abortive French invasion at Bantry Bay in 1796. There are also lots of model boats and other knick-knacks, as well as a giant optic that once served as the light of the Bailey Lighthouse at Howth.

● *Just beside the Maritime Museum, in Moran Park, is a remarkable statue of 'Christ the King' by Andrew O'Connor, constructed as a memorial to all those who died in the First World War. It was bought for the park in 1949, but was kept out of sight for several decades, until Dun Laoghaire was deemed to be ready for it.*

James Joyce Museum and the Forty Foot

Sandycove, Dun Laoghaire, **T** 01 280 9265, www.visitdublin.com
Apr-Oct, Mon-Sat 1000-1300, 1400-1700, Sun and public holidays 1400-1800. Closed Nov-Mar. €6. DART Sandycove.   Map 7, p256

It's a bracing walk from the harbour at Dun Laoghaire to the Joyce Museum at Sandycove. On the way you'll pass a small, sandy beach and the **Forty Foot** bathing place, named not for the depth of the water, but after the regiment that was once stationed here. For many years, the Forty Foot was for gentlemen only: female eyes never sullied the strictly male atmosphere, and a sign at the water's edge proclaimed 'No dogs, no togs'. Nowadays togs are compulsory, although you might see the odd naked torso or two a little further round the coast. The Forty Foot features prominently in *At Swim, Two Boys* (p231), so fans of the novel will have a special reason to visit.

Behind the Forty Foot is the Martello tower, built as a look-out during the Napoleonic Wars and immortalized in the opening chapter of *Ulysses*. James Joyce actually stayed here for a short time in 1904, until one of his companions shot at him while sleepwalking, convincing Joyce that it was time to decamp. The tower now houses a small museum containing original manuscripts, letters, personal items such as his waistcoat, guitar and piano, as well as a death mask of the author made in January 1945. The basic living room has been arranged in the way Joyce described it, and there are some good views from the roof.

Dalkey Castle and Heritage Centre

Castle St, Dalkey, **T** 01 285 8366, www.dalkeycastle.com *Apr-Dec, Mon-Fri 0930-1700, Sat and Sun 1100-1700, Jan-Mar, Sat, Sun and public holidays 1100-1700. €7. DART Dalkey. Bus 7D (from O'Connell St), 59 (from Dun Laoghaire). Map 7, p256*

South of Sandycove, the tiny seaside village of Dalkey boasts the highest house prices in Ireland thanks to an influx of rich folk and celebs. Homes in one particular street, **Sorrento Terrace**, have changed hands for a king's ransom. However, Dalkey has more to offer than the thrill of spotting a member of U2, not least its amazing views of Dublin Bay and its excellent sandy beaches. The village itself is ancient and once served as Dublin's main port, as testified by the presence of Goat, Bullock and Archbold's castles, three remaining 15th-century tower houses of seven that once protected the village.

Impressive **Goat Castle** – complete with murder hole and battlements – now houses the village heritage centre, with exhibitions on the history of Dalkey from its earliest times to the present, including details of the quarry that provided granite for the harbour walls at Dun Laoghaire. The centre also suggests the possible route taken by Stephen Dedalus in Joyce's *Ulysses*, from the tower at Sandycove to the school on Dalkey Avenue at which he taught in the novel. Surrounding the castle, **St Begnet's** churchyard has ruins dating back to the ninth century.

Heritage walks are offered in the summer, but you can also strike out on your own along Vico Road above the shore, past the quarry and up onto the open ground of the hills, before descending towards **Killiney**. This is another pretty, superstar-saturated village with its own DART station to take you back to the city.

● *Just offshore, Dalkey Island is home to a Martello tower, the remains of an oratory, some rare birds and a herd of goats. You can hire a boat out to the island from the harbour.*

Bray
DART Bray. Map 7, p256

The once-lively seaside resort of Bray, with its terraces of stern Victorian boarding houses, stony beach, long promenade and tired amusement arcades, is strangely romantic in low season. The main tourist attraction is the **National Sea Life Centre** (p206), which offers close encounters with shrimps and sharks, cuckoo wrasse and catfish, and other species found in Irish waters. A leaflet detailing an architectural walk around the town can be picked up from the tourist office in the old courthouse on Main Street (**T** 01 286 6796). Most appealing, however, is the soul-uplifting coastal walk along 8 km (5 miles) of clifftop pathways that thread their way south from the end of the esplanade. Alternatively, climb **Bray Head** (it's about an hour to the top and back) for views of the Wicklow Hills and all the way to Wales on a clear day.

Kilruddery House and Gardens
Between Bray and Greystones, **T** 01 286 2777. *House May, Jun and Sep, daily 1300-1700, closed Oct-Apr and July, Aug. Gardens May-Sep, daily 1300-1700, closed Oct-Apr. Map 7, p256*

Distinguished by twin canals and a gorgeous avenue of lime trees, the grounds at Kilruddery near Bray incorporate the largest surviving French-style garden in Ireland. It is regarded as one of the most significant 17th-century gardens still in existence in the British Isles, and is a must-see for green-fingered visitors.

North of Dublin

*There are some appealing places to visit north of the city, and most of them can be easily reached by train from the centre of Dublin. **Howth** combines a working harbour, a transport museum and one of the best clifftop walks in Ireland. Further north, sandy white* *beaches and dunes dominated by golf courses stretch towards* **Malahide**. *Buzzing with activity during the rush hours, but descending into a quiet doze in between, this attractive commuter town is where well-heeled Dubliners spend their evenings away from the fuss of the city. It's* **Malahide Castle** *that's the big draw for tourists though, with the* **Fry Model Railway** *and the* **Talbot Botanic Gardens** *in its grounds. If you've time to spare, consider spending a night in* **Skerries** *to make the most of the village's beachside walks, music pubs and working mills, and to visit a nearby stately home that is open to the public. Further afield again is the world-famous* **Newgrange** *passage tomb, perhaps best visited as part of an organized tour from Dublin, if only to take the hassle out of getting there.*

▸▸ *See Sleeping p122, Eating and drinking p146*

 ## Sights

Howth
DART Howth. Map 7, p256

Howth is situated 15 km (9 miles) northeast of the city at the end of the lumpy peninsula that forms the northern portion of Dublin Bay. Popular with yacht owners and home to a small fishing fleet, this quiet little town has a very long history; the ancient geographer Ptolemy even included it on one of his maps. In the village are the **National Transport Museum** and the 15th-century ruins of **St Mary's Abbey**, which was founded in 1042. The highlight of a visit to Howth, however, is the stunning hillside and coastal walk around **Howth Head**, which is a fulfilling way to spend a bright afternoon.

● *Off the coast at Howth is Ireland's Eye, an island bird sanctuary that shelters puffins and other species, as well as a sixth-century monastery. Boats to the island depart from Howth's east pier from 1100 daily during the summer,* **T** *01 831 4200.*

A way a lone a last a loved a long
the riverrun, past Eve and Adam's,
from swerve of shore to bend of bay,
brings us by a commodius vicus of recirculation
back to Howth Castle and Environs.

*The closing and opening words
of Finnegan's Wake by James Joyce*

A walk around Howth Head

From Howth DART station cross the road, go through the gap in the wall and follow the steps and footpath to Grace O'Malley Drive. Turn right, follow the road for a little way, and then turn right between some houses into a street called Balkil Park and on through a fence onto some open land. Head south and uphill towards the mobile phone transmitter at the summit, from where there are exhilarating views. You can wander about the hillside and golf courses up here, but if you want a more challenging walk, head west and down the hill, following the line of white-painted stones along well-marked pathways as far as Carrickbrack Road. Turn right and look for a sign on the seaward side indicating a dangerous cliff edge. Make your way towards it and you will find yourself on the Howth Head cliff walk. Turn to your left and spend the rest of the afternoon walking along the coast all the way back to Howth village.

National Transport Museum

Heritage Depot, Howth Castle Demesne, **T** 01 848 0831, www.nationaltransportmuseum.org *Sep-May, Sat, Sun and bank holidays 1400-1700, Jun-Aug, daily 1000-1700. €3. DART Howth. Map 7, p256*

Sixty trams, buses, lorries, fire engines and army vehicles, dating from the late-19th century through to the later years of the 20th century are on display in an exhibition space just inside the gates of Howth Castle. Among the exhibits is the Dublin tram that once ran up Howth Hill. The castle, which has been owned by the St Lawrence family continuously for eight centuries, is closed to the public, but the grounds are worth exploring, especially in May when the rhododendrons are in full bloom.

Malahide Castle

Malahide Castle Demesne, Malahide, **T** 01 846 2184. *Castle tours Mon-Sat 1000-1245 and 1400-1700, Sun and public holidays 1100-1245 and 1400-1700. Fry Model Railway and Tara's Palace, Apr-Sep, Mon-Sat 1000-1300 and 1400-1700, Sun and public holidays 1400-1800. Castle tour €6. Fry Model Railway €2. DART/suburban rail Malahide. Bus 42 (from Beresford Place).* Map 7, p256

Set in a lovely 250-acre (506-ha) estate, this three-storey fortified house was owned for nearly 800 years by the Talbot family, apart from a brief period during the English interregnum. When the last Talbot died in 1975, Dublin Council bought the property and opened it to the public. The original 12th-century building is all gone, but one tiny part of a tower (closed to the public) dates back to the 14th century. The excellent tour of the house is the only way to see the interior, which is full of the family's original possessions and other objects that also seem to have become part of the place. Instead of high-tech audio-visual displays, there is pleasing evidence of the way the house was actually used by the Talbot family. There are pretty turrets at each corner of the building that served as dressing rooms, sun rooms or bathrooms, a worn-out looking library and a massive collection of family portraits.

Housed in an outbuilding in the castle grounds, **Fry Model Railway**, **T** 01 846 3779, is the train set to beat all train sets. It was collected by Cyril Fry, a railway engineer, and reproduces the Irish rail system in minute detail. In fact, the only thing that seems to be missing is dried-up sandwiches in the buffet cars. Also here is

!

Grace O'Malley, the 16th-century pirate queen, is said to have been refused dinner and a bed at Howth Castle. In retaliation, she kidnapped one of the children, holding him captive until the St Lawrences promised to show traditional hospitality towards future guests. Ever since, the family has set an extra place at the table for any unexpected visitors.

Tara's Palace, a collection of doll's houses and dolls dominated by the eponymous mansion constructed by Ron and Doreen McDonnell in 1980. It is based on Leinster House and comes complete with tiny silverware, paintings, cutlery and curtains.

On the other side of the castle are the 20-acre **Talbot Botanic Gardens**, planted between 1948 and 1973 by Milo Talbot, the last member of the family to own the castle. The gardens contain over 5,000 species of exotic plants from around the world.

Skerries Watermills and Windmill

Skerries, **T** 01 849 5208, http://indigo.ie/~skerries *Apr-Sep, daily 1030-1730, Oct-Mar, daily 1030-1630. Closed 20 Dec-1 Jan and Good Friday. €5. Suburban rail Skerries. Bus 33 (from Eden Quay). Map 7, p256*

Skerries is an unintentionally picturesque fishing village-cum-commuter town that's worth a day's visit for its beach walks, sea views, thatched cottages, music pubs and a couple of excellent restaurants. Right in the centre of the village is a mill complex dating back to the 16th century that was once owned by the Priory Canons of St Augustine. The bakery came into being some time around 1840. You can watch the restored mills in action, try a bit of milling yourself and sample some of the tasty baked products in the café.

● *At the very end of the tombolo of land that makes up Skerries is a spit of sand known locally as Red Island. It's a great spot for a picnic.*

Ardgillan Demesne

Balbriggan, **T** 01 849 2212. *Apr-Jun and Sep, Tue-Sun and public holidays 1100-1800, Oct-Mar, Tue-Sun and public holidays 1100-1630, Jul and Aug, daily 1100-1800. Closed 23 Dec-1 Jan. €4. Tours of the gardens Thu 1530. Bus 33 (from Eden Quay or Skerries). Map 7, p256*

A half-hour walk or brief bus ride out of Skerries on the coast road brings you to this grand old house, which enjoys one of the most spectacular settings of any country estate in Ireland. Located on a hillside with panoramic views of the sea to the east and the Mourne Mountains to the north, this is not so much a castle as a castellated 18th-century house that was extended from relatively modest beginnings to provide servants' quarters and estate offices. The demesne was originally owned by the Gaelic O'Casey family, but they seem to have lost the estate during the British interregnum, and by 1738, when the present house was built, Ardgillan was owned by a family called Taylor. Dublin Council acquired the estate in the 1980s and set about restoring the house, according to 19th-century style.

For those who tire of great drawing rooms, the most enjoyable area to visit is the kitchen, which has been carefully restored to working order; the stone sink in the scullery still shows the marks where some poor scullery maid scrubbed away at the Taylors' grand gowns and bedlinen.

There's plenty to see in the grounds, too, including a heated glasshouse, a Victorian rose garden, a walled garden, 8 km (5 miles) of footpaths and two coffee shops. An ice house, once used to store perishables, was recently discovered and there are also plans for a museum of garden history.

★ Newgrange Passage Tomb

Domore, **T** 041 982 0300. *Jun-mid Sep 0900-1900, May and late Sep, daily 0900-1830, Mar, Apr and Oct, daily 0930-1730, Nov-Feb, daily 0930-1700. Visitor centre €3, passage grave plus visitor centre €5. Bus Éireann from Busáras daily 0900, 1000, 1100, 1330, 1415, 1500 (last bus departs Domore Mon-Sat 1605, Sun 1525).* Map 7, p256

The spectacular Neolithic burial site at Newgrange is the mythological home of the Tuatha de Danainn, a subterranean race of supernatural beings dedicated to the goddess Danu.

It was only in 1699 that the central tomb was accidentally discovered. A passageway runs for 62 ft (10 m) from the tomb entrance to the central cavern, sloping upwards, so that in normal circumstances, sunlight shining into the grave only reaches about halfway along the passage. However, the prehistoric builders of Newgrange also inserted a 'roof box' above the entrance, so that when the sun rises on the shortest day of the year a sliver of light penetrates all the way to the central chamber. This only occurs around the winter solstice, and even then only for a maximum of 17 minutes in the morning. Newgrange is closed to members of the public on the solstice itself, but the guided tour simulates the effect at other times of year to give visitors some idea of this magical experience.

The geometric motifs that decorate the interior stones give credence to the idea that Newgrange was far more than just a burial place for some important ruling clan. Lozenge and zigzag designs, and especially the double and triple spiral patterns, have never been interpreted to everyone's satisfaction, so your guess as to their meaning is as valid as most. What remains undisputed, however, is the sense of awe generated by viewing finely executed stone carving that was chiselled by craftspeople over 5,000 years ago. Inside the central chamber, the most spectacular sight is the roof, whose every stone rests on the twin halves of the stones underneath to dizzyingly angular effect. This feat of engineering has kept the chamber bone dry for millennia and is unrivalled in the ancient world.

Visits to Newgrange are via the Brú na Bóinne Visitor Centre at Domore, from where a shuttle bus takes you to the passage grave and on to a similar tomb at Knowth. In summer, delays are caused by the sheer numbers of visitors and by limited access to the chambers, so go early in the morning if you don't want to wait, or delay your visit until the low season – either way, it's worth it.

The choice of accommodation in Dublin ranges from elegant luxury hotels to dormitory beds in hostels with self-catering kitchens. Breakfast (either continental or full Irish) is usually included in the room price, although expensive hotels and some hostels may charge extra. Hotels are graded according to a star system by Dublin Tourism, with prices from around €100 per night for a decent three-star choice to more than €450 for the very best accommodation in the city. Single person supplements are standard and can be exorbitant. However, rates are often cheaper in low season, and may be negotiable at other times of year depending on demand, particularly if you stay for more than one night, make a dinner reservation at the hotel or book a family room. You should also look out for special deals offered by airline companies or when booking online.

Always confirm the price of your room before making a reservation and always try to make your booking in advance, especially during holiday periods, festivals or big sporting events, p173.

€ Sleeping codes

Price

LL	€450 and over	C	€150-190
L	€320-450	D	€80-150
AL	€290-320	E	€60-80
A	€240-290	F	€25-60
B	€190-240	G	€25 and under

The prices refer to the cost of a double room, or in the case of hostels, two beds in a dorm room. Check-in times in the city centre is often 1400, and check-out time is usually midday.

In general, the most expensive and upmarket hotels are located south of the river, especially in the Grafton Street area, while affordable two-star hotels and guesthouses with character are clustered around Gardiner Street on the north side. If you want to avoid the weekend crowds, choose a hotel out of the town centre at Ballsbridge, Dun Laoghaire, or even further afield. Bear in mind, though, that accommodation in Ballsbridge tends to be pricey, especially when compared to guesthouses and B&Bs in Gardiner Street or in the northern suburb of Clontarf.

The distinction between a guesthouse and a small hotel is often fairly academic, with most guesthouses now offering en suite rooms with TVs, direct-dial phones and tea- and coffee-making facilities, plus a lounge and, occasionally, a bar. A guesthouse breakfast may be far better and more individually prepared than what's on offer in a hotel. A typical city B&B will be a small, owner-occupied house with two or three bedrooms set aside for guests; not all rooms will have their own bathroom.

If you're on a tight budget but you don't want to sleep in a dormitory, the most economical choice may be a private room in a hostel. Check out www.hostels.com, which provides information and takes bookings for hostel and budget accommodation in Dublin.

Grafton Street and around

Hotels

LL-AL **Conrad Dublin**, Earlsfort Terrace, **T** 01 602 8900, **F** 01 676 5424, www.conradhotels.com *Map 2, F8, p249* Close to St Stephen's Green and the city's finest restaurants, this place has been recently refurbished in classy modern style and has every mod con that the discerning traveller needs to unwind from a hard day's sightseeing.

L **The Merrion**, Merrion St Upper, **T** 01 603 0600, **F** 01 603 0700, www.merrionhotel.com *Map 2, D9, p249* The Merrion is the ultimate in understated luxury in the heart of the city. Four converted Georgian houses – one was the birthplace of the Duke of Wellington – plus a new block in the same style, surround pretty formal gardens. Spacious, comfortable rooms are supplemented by two restaurants, a pool and a fitness centre, and there's an impressive collection of art scattered around the serene interiors.

C **Trinity Capital**, Pearse St, **T** 01 648 1000, **F** 01 648 1010, www.capital-hotels.com *Map 2, A9, p249* A newish, fashionable hotel in a quiet area between Trinity College and the river, the Trinity Capital offers outlandish décor, comfortable rooms, free entrance to Fireworks nightclub on the corner and a key card to get you into more than half a dozen other pubs and clubs around the city for free. Good breakfasts, too.

C-D **Camden Court Hotel**, Camden St, **T** 01 475 9666, **F** 01 475 9677, www.camdencourthotel.com *Map 2, G6, p248* Located amid the quaint shops and music pubs of the 'village quarter', this huge, modern hotel is thankfully away from the street noise of late-night clubbers but remains close enough to all the sights.

Sleeping

★ Hostels

sidebar
Best

- Avalon House, p108
- Four Courts, p111
- Brewery Hostel, p111
- Dublin International Youth Hostel, p118
- Marina House, p122

sidebar
Sleeping

Best of all, it has its own leisure centre and pool where you can work off all the extra calories you may have consumed at the carvery in the popular Pishogues bar. Secure car parking for hotel guests is a bonus.

C-D Mercer Hotel, Mercer St Lower, **T** 01 478 3677, **F** 01 478 0328, www.mercerhotel.ie *Map 2, D6, p248* With a very central location off Grafton Street, this new, middle-range hotel is far enough out of Temple Bar to afford some peace at night, but still has easy access to shops and city centre sights.

Guesthouses and B&Bs

D Baggot Court, 92 Baggot St Lower, **T** 01 661 2819, baggot@indigo.ie *Map 2, E11, p249* Close to the centre in a quiet area of the city, the Baggot Court has pleasantly appointed rooms, albeit identically furnished in pine, each with bath and shower. There's also a small lounge area for guest use, and, more importantly, off-street parking.

D Kilronan Guesthouse 70 Adelaide Rd, **T** 01 475 5266, **F** 01 478 2841, www.dublin.com *Map 2, G7, p249* This award-winning guesthouse can rival most small hotels for its high standards of service and comfort. It also has a private car park.

★ Top-notch hotels

Best

- The Merrion, p106
- The Clarence, p109
- Four Seasons, p111
- The Towers, p112
- The Morrison, p115

Hostels

D-F Ashfield House, 19/20 D'Olier St, **T** 01 679 7734, **F** 01 679 0852, www.ashfield@indigo.ie *Map 2, A8, p249* Close to Trinity College, this place has dorm beds, family rooms and twin rooms, all en suite. Breakfast included.

E-F Avalon House, 55 Aungier St, **T** 01 475 0001, **F** 01 475 0303, www.avalon-house.ie *Map 2, D5, p248* This hostel has been recently extended and refurbished. It offers dorm accommodation in spacious, well-designed rooms, with unisex toilets and shower rooms, plus single-sex dorms, en suite singles and doubles, and a self-contained double room with a small kitchen and en suite shower for less than €80. Breakfast included.

Self-catering

C Molesworth Court Suites, 35 Schoolhouse Lane, Kildare St, **T** 01 676 4799, **F** 01 676 4982, www.molesworthcourt.i.e *Map 2, F9, p249* Central serviced apartments with up to three bedrooms.

D Trinity College, **T** 01 608 1177. *16 Jun-3 Oct*. *Map 2, A8, p249* Single en suite rooms in shared apartments, plus kitchens, bar, laundry, sports facilities and car park. Breakfast included.

★ **Guesthouses**

Best
- Aberdeen House, p112
- Anglesea House, p113
- Ariel House, p113
- Merrion Hall, p113
- Redbank Guesthouse, p123

Temple Bar and around

Hotels

L **The Clarence**, 6-8 Wellington Quay, **T** 01 407 0800, **F** 01 407 0820, www.theclarence.ie *Map 3, C4, p250* Originally built in 1852 and now owned by U2, as someone will no doubt inform you sooner or later, this venerable old hotel has preserved its original wood panelling amid many modish embellishments: leather-clad lifts, CD players (but no tea- and coffee-making facilities) in the individually designed bedrooms and Egyptian cotton on the king-size beds. The decor is enlivened by rich colours and Irish craftwork; friendly staff wearing designer outfits that look vaguely clerical, and a bookless lounge called the Study has original artwork on the walls. All this contributes to the hotel's strange mix of the spartan and the self-indulgent.

B **Paramount Hotel**, Parliament St and Essex Gate, **T** 01 417 9900, **F** 01 417 9904, www.paramounthotel.ie *Map 3, D3, p250* Temple Bar's only quiet street is now home to this recently built labyrinthine place. It has large comfortable rooms, several of which look out onto an internal courtyard, offering a quiet night amid the hubbub of the area. Breakfast can get very busy, so be prepared to get up before the carousers if you want to eat in peace. Downstairs

★ **Mid-range hotels**

Best

- Paramount Hotel, p109
- Jury's Inn Christchurch, p110
- Bewley's Ballsbridge, p112
- Academy Hotel, p115
- Castle Hotel, p115

is the Turk's Head bar for those who want a short stagger back to their bedrooms; you may even catch sight of the belly dancer who livens the place up now and again.

D Jury's Inn Christchurch, Christchurch Place, **T** 01 454 0000, **F** 01 454 0012, www.bookajurysinn.com *Map 3, F1, p250* Jury's comfortable rooms will accommodate three adults, or two adults and two children, making them good value for families or groups, although breakfast is not included in the room rate. There's secure parking, a pub with live music and an informal restaurant on site.

Hostels

E Barnacles, Temple Bar House, 19 Temple Lane, **T** 01 671 6277, **F** 01 671 6591, www.tbh@barnacles.ie *Map 3, C6, p250* All singles, doubles, family rooms and dorms are en suite. There's also an attractive modern lounge area, good security, a left luggage facility and safes for guest use. Breakfast is included.

E-F Gogarty's Temple Bar Hostel, 18-21 Anglesea St, **T** 01 671 1822, **F** 01 671 7637, www.olivergogarty.com *Map 3, C7, p250* In the very epicentre of all the fun of Temple Bar, this hostel offers private doubles and dormitory rooms, all en suite, plus storage for bicycles, internet access and secure parking. Breakfast is included.

E-F **Kinlay House**, 2-12 Lord Edward St, **T** 01 679 6644, **F** 01 679 7437, www.kinlay-dublin@usitworld.com *Map 3, E2, p250* Although it's outside Temple Bar proper, this hostel can still be noisy at night. It has dorm beds, single and double rooms (some en suite) and unisex bathrooms. Breakfast is included.

The Liberties and west

Hostels

E-F **Four Courts Hostel**, 15-17 Merchant's Quay, **T** 01 672 5839, **F** 01 672 5862, info@fourcourtshostel.com *Map 2, A3, p248* South of the river with views of the Four Courts, this hostel has got its act together to offer stylish dorms and private rooms. It also boasts a lounge area, pool table, good kitchens, internet access and a non-smoking reading room with tourist literature. No curfew.

F **Brewery Hostel**, 22/25 Thomas St, **T** 01 453 8600, **F** 01 453 8616, brewery@indigo.ie *Map 2, B1, p248* This family-run hostel is close to the Guinness Storehouse and Heuston Station in a tourist-free area of town. Open all year, it has over 50 dorm beds and five private doubles, plus a paved area at the back with picnic tables. There are some lively pubs and clubs nearby.

Ballsbridge and south

Hotels

LL-L **Four Seasons**, Simmonscourt Rd, **T** 01 665 4000, **F** 01 665 4099, www.fourseasons.com *Map 4, F6, p251* The Four Seasons is a very luxurious hotel, with huge public areas, neoclassical decor and attentive staff. The large bedrooms and suites would be spacious enough to accommodate a small commune. Silver service sets the tone in the genteel, roomy restaurant, which looks out on to a garden courtyard and the sleek new Ice Bar attracts the city's coolest thirtysomethings. A place to spoil yourself.

L-AL Jury's Ballsbridge/The Towers, Lansdowne Rd, **T** 01 660 5000 (Ballsbridge), **T** 01 667 0033 (Towers), **F** 01 660 5540 (Ballsbridge), **F** 01 667 2595 (Towers), www.jurysdoyle.com *Map 4, D3, p251* This large, friendly hotel has spacious bedrooms, an indoor/outdoor pool and gym, free parking and a good choice of eating and drinking options. Attached but separate is The Towers, eight floors of air-conditioned luxury rooms, with a cool hospitality lounge and exclusive breakfast area. Guests can enjoy complimentary evening cocktails, all-day cappuccinos, plus all the sociable fun of the main hotel next door.

D Bewley's Hotel Ballsbridge, Merrion Rd, **T** 01 668 1111, **F** 01 668 1999, www.bewleyshotels.com *Map 4, F6, p251* At around €99 for up to three adults or a family of four, Bewley's smart, spacious and comfortable bedrooms represent excellent value, especially in the Ballsbridge area. The red-brick Victorian building has been converted from a convent school and the original entrance way opens into a roomy public area. Downstairs is the quality O'Connell's restaurant, as well as a café.

Guesthouses

D Aberdeen Lodge, 53 Park Ave, **T** 01 283 8155, **F** 01 283 7877, www.halpinsprivatehotels.com *Map 4, G9, p251* As well as one of the best breakfasts in Dublin, this luxurious Edwardian guesthouse offers tea and biscuits on arrival, and hot drinks throughout the day. Hotel-standard bedrooms are complemented by an elegant lounge area and gardens overlooking the cricket ground. A value-for-money alternative to congested city-centre hotels.

D **Anglesea House**, 63 Anglesea Rd, **T** 01 668 3877. *Map 4, F4, p251* A well-run establishment in a quiet side street, Anglesea House is Ballsbridge gentility at its best, with personal service and lots of charm. There are seven individually furnished en-suite rooms, a huge lounge with library and a sunny breakfast room. The exemplary breakfast includes home-baked pastries, specially prepared cereal and amazing omelettes. There's off-street parking and city centre buses stop five-minutes' walk away.

D **Ariel House**, 52 Lansdowne Rd, **T** 01 668 5512, www.ariel-house.com *Map 4, B4, p251* Built in the 1860s, this listed, red-brick building is a classy guesthouse with a choice of no-smoking rooms. All have bath and shower, while three boast four-poster beds. North Americans, justifiably, adore the decor and antiques. Ariel House is three minutes on foot from Lansdowne Road DART station and has its own car park.

D **Merrion Hall**, 56 Merrion Rd, **T** 01 668 1426, www.halpinsprivatehotels.com *Map 4, E5, p251* A quiet welcoming place with four-poster beds, an ample lounge area, private gardens and a library of tourist literature. Award-winning breakfasts are served in the serene, sunny breakfast room.

B&Bs

E **Oaklodge**, 4 Pembroke Park, **T** 01 660 6096, www.oaklodge.ie *Map 4, F1, p251* This Victorian terraced house has four bedrooms (three en suite), each with a TV and tea- and coffee-making facilities. Family friendly but no child reductions.

E-F **Carmel Chambers**, 25 Anglesea Rd, **T/F** 01 668 7346. *Map 4, E4, p251* Close to city centre bus routes and some good local restaurants, this B&B has one en-suite bedroom, plus single, double and triple rooms. Reasonable value for this area.

E-F St Dunstan's, 25A Oakley Rd, Ranelagh, **T** 01 497 2286.
A little out of town but convenient for bus and DART services, this
Edwardian townhouse has three no-smoking double rooms with
TV and tea- and coffee-making facilities.

O'Connell Street and around

Hotels

B Clarion Hotel Dublin IFSC, Excise Walk, **T** 01 433 8800, **F** 01
433 8801, info@clarionhotelifsc.ie *Map 1, D6, p247* The Clarion
is a shiny new hotel, set in the shiny new IFSC area of the city,
overlooking the Liffey. Riveting industrial river scapes are on view
from the windows of the fresh, big, uncluttered rooms, and the
new docks development provides plenty of sandwich bars,
restaurants and clubs nearby. The hotel has a fitness centre and
pool, and the bar serves Asian fusion food. Neat breakfast.

B Gresham, 25 O'Connell St Upper, **T** 01 874 6881, **F** 01 878
7175, www.gresham-hotels.com *Map 5, F7, p253* The Gresham
claims to have the highest ratio of porters to rooms in Ireland.
Close to the GPO, the hotel has a very colourful past: it was
destroyed by British shelling in 1916, hosted the Irish Nazi party's
last annual Christmas get-together before the outbreak of World
War II and withstood Beatle-mania in the 1960s. The elegiac
closing scene of Joyce's 'The Dead' was also set in one of the
hotel's 288 spacious guest rooms.

! An urban myth tells how a Dublin character known as Bird
Flanagan once rode a horse through the swing doors of the
Gresham hotel and up to the bar. When the barman refused
to serve him because it was after hours, Flanagan replied:
"It's not for me you fool, it's for the horse."

B **The Morrison**, 15 Ormond Quay, **T** 01 887 2400, **F** 01 878 3185, www.morrisonhotel.ie *Map 3, B4, p250* Part of the gentrification of North Dublin, this classy designer building sits unobtrusively on the banks of the Liffey and vies with The Clarence as Dublin's hippest hotel. New-fashioned decor in black, white and brown is refreshingly un-Irish, and is supplemented by mood lighting, CD-players in the rooms, complimentary tea and coffee on request, and dried things in big glass bowls. Breakfast is not included in the room rate. The hotel restaurant, Halo, is renowned as one of the city's most stylish places to eat (p141).

C-D **Academy Hotel**, Findlater Place, **T** 01 878 0666, **F** 01 878 0600, www.academy-hotel.com *Map 5, F7, p253* The Academy enjoys a useful central location just off O'Connell St but away from all the fuss. It's busy, but still attentive to customers, with bright, modern, well-equipped rooms, a pleasant buffet breakfast and very reasonable rates. Secure parking is available.

C-D **Lynam's Hotel**, 63/64 O'Connell St, **T** 01 888 0886, **F** 01 888 0890, www.lynams-hotel.com *Map 5, G7, p253* The two Georgian houses that make up Lynam's Hotel were once owned by the inventor of the tilley lamp. Although they're bang in the centre of O'Connell Street, the 42 smart and modern bedrooms are not noisy. Inside, the comfortable lounge area on the first floor overlooks the main drag, and the recently improved lobby has a small café at the rear.

D **Castle Hotel**, 3-4 Gt Denmark St, **T** 01 874 6949, **F** 01 872 7674, hotels@indigo.ie *Map 5, E6, p252* The Castle is one of our favourites: a lovingly restored Georgian building that offers so much more (at a better price) than some of the faceless hotels around town. There's an elegant lounge area, comfortable bedrooms and car parking for guests. (Michael Collins used room 201 as one of his safe houses during the War of Independence.)

D Jury's Inn Custom House, Custom House Quay , **T** 01 607 5000, **F** 01 829 0400, www.bookajurysinn.com *Map 5, H11, p253* Set on the riverside near O'Connell Street, this hotel charges a flat room rate of around €96 per night (check the website for deals), except during rugby weekends when the price rockets. Breakfast in the self-service cafeteria is not included. Front rooms boast views of the river and the Wicklow Hills, but back rooms are quieter.

D Walton's Hotel, 2-5 North Frederick St, **T** 01 878 3131, **F** 01 878 3090, waltonshotel@eircom.net *Map 5, D6, p252* It looks like any other small hotel from the outside, but Walton's turns out to be a carefully renovated Georgian building. The lounge is a treat, with paintings of Michael Collins and other Republicans on the walls. Comfortable bedrooms (including singles), a car park and friendly, efficient staff all make Walton's a very decent choice.

Guesthouses

C-D Glen Guesthouse, 84 Gardiner St Lower, **T** 01 855 1374, theglen@eircom.net *Map 5, F8, p253* This small, 12-room guesthouse occupies a well-restored Georgian building in a central but quiet location. Reasonable rates.

C-E Clifden Guesthouse, 32 Gardiner Place, **T** 01 874 6364, www.clifdenhouse.com *Map 5, D7, p253* A fair spread of rooms including singles, doubles, triple rooms and family rooms. Breakfast is extra, but parking is free.

C-E Comfort Inn, 95-98 Talbot St, **T** 01 874 9202, **F** 01 874 9672, www.comfort-inn-dublin.com *Map 5, G8, p253* This refurbished, professional guesthouse has the atmosphere and amenities of a small hotel, and enjoys a good location for sightseeing. There are 48 smartly furnished bedrooms, plus a congenial lounge area and an outdoor patio for picnic meals. Rates do not include breakfast.

D Georgian Court Guesthouse, 77 Gardiner St Lower, **T** 01 855 7872, georgiancourt@eircom.net *Map 5, F9, p253* Triple and family rooms as well as doubles are offered at this converted Georgian terraced house. En-suite rooms have showers, not baths. There's also a comfortable, roomy lounge area and secure parking. It's popular in summer, so advance booking is essential.

F Marian Guesthouse, 21 Gardiner St Upper, **T** 01 874 4129. *Map 5, C7, p253* This fair-value, family-run guesthouse offers standard rooms at B&B prices. It's close to Mountjoy Square and bus no 14 from the airport stops nearby.

Hostels

D-E Globetrotters Tourist Hostel, 46-8 Gardiner St Lower, **T** 01 873 5893, **F** 01 878 8787. *Map 5, G9, p253* More of a guesthouse with a kitchen, the Globetrotters is one of the most expensive hostels in Dublin if you opt for a private room. Rates include breakfast.

D-G Isaac's Hostel, 2-5 Frenchman's Lane, **T** 01 855 6215, **F** 01 855 6574, www.isaacs.ie *Map 5, G9, p253* Next to Busáras, this noisy but sociable place has the cheapest dorm beds in the city, as well as more expensive private rooms. Hostel amenities include internet access, a tiny deli, safes and a left-luggage facility. Guests should note that rooms are closed between 1130 and 1430 each day for cleaning.

E-F Abbey Court, 29 Bachelor's Walk, **T** 01 878 0700, **F** 01 878 0719, www.abbey-court.com *Map 5, H7, p253* Centrally located beside O'Connell Bridge, Abbey Court is a newish hostel with private doubles and dormitory accommodation. All rooms have en-suite power showers. Rates include continental breakfast and there's also an outdoor barbecue area. Key card access.

E-F Jacob's Inn, 21-28 Talbot Place, **T** 01 855 5660, **F** 01 855 5664, www.isaacs.ie *Map 5, F10, p253* Jacob's Inn offers en suite private rooms and dorm beds, plus a café-style restaurant, internet access, free left-luggage facility, TV lounge and safes. It's located in a quiet road off O'Connell Street. One- and two-bedroom serviced apartments are also available in an adjoining purpose-built block. The apartments sleep up to five people and can be rented by the week for €500-750.

F Dublin International Youth Hostel, 61 Mountjoy St, **T** 01 830 1766, www.iyhf.org *Map 5, D5, p252* Housed in a renovated convent, this Óige (Hostelling International) hostel has multi-bed accommodation, a few double rooms, a huge kitchen, TV room, secure parking and a brilliant dining room in the old chapel. Check out the phones in the old confessional boxes. Supplement for non-members.

G Litton Lane Hostel, 2-4 Litton Lane, **T** 01 872 8389, **F** 01 872 0039, litton@indigo.ie *Map 3, A7, p250* There are only three private rooms in this relatively new hostel. Once a recording studio, the building now also houses a laundry and a trendy café. Breakfast included.

From Smithfield to the Phoenix Park

Hotels

B-D Ashling Hotel, Parkgate St, **T** 01 677 2324, **F** 01 679 3785, www.ashlinghotel.ie *Map 6, F10, p255* The Ashling Hotel is worth considering for any package deals that might be available. Close to Heuston Station and the Phoenix Park, the hotel has great views of the river Liffey and of the rising curls of alcoholic steam from the Guinness brewery on the opposite bank. There are bus stops nearby for access to the town centre. The philosopher Wittgenstein stayed here while writing parts of his *Philosophical Investigations* in 1948.

B-D **Chief O'Neill's**, Smithfield Village, **T** 01 817 3838, **F** 01 817 3839, www.chiefoneills.com *Map 5, H2, p252* In the centre of reconstructed Smithfield Village, this modern hotel successfully strives to be different, with frosted green glass and modish lighting. The bedrooms have CD players, kettles and nifty sinks, and there's a café-bar downstairs. Rates do not include breakfast. If you are fed up with anonymous, all-too-similar hotels, consider staying here. The Cobblestone, one of the best music pubs in the city, is located nearby, p157.

Guesthouses

D-E **Phoenix Park House**, 38-9 Parkgate St, **T** 01 677 2870, **F** 01 679 9769, www.dublinguesthouse.com *Map 6, F10, p255* Taking its name from the nearby Phoenix Park, this large, family-run place is located beside Ryan's bar in a quiet area of town. Buses for the city centre stop nearby.

Glasnevin and Clontarf

Hotels

A **Clontarf Castle Hotel**, Castle Ave, Clontarf, **T** 01 833 2321, **F** 01 833 0418, info@clontarfcastle.ie *Map 1, A9, p247* Well off the beaten track of swanky hotels, this is a gloriously reconstructed version of the fortified house that was originally built here in 1172. In addition to the large-scale lobby, communal areas include the King's Table restaurant and two bars.

B&Bs

E Aghadoe House, 77 Botanic Rd, Glasnevin, **T** 01 830 0466, www.aghadoehouse.com *Map 1, A4, p247* Four en suite bedrooms are offered on a busy part of Botanic Road, near Iona Road. There's a bus stop close by and parking is available.

E Botanic View, 25 Botanic Rd, Glasnevin, **T** 01 860 0195, **F** 01 830 5275, botanic@indigo.ie *Map 1, A4, p247* Standard B&B accommodation in four en suite rooms. Car parking.

E Botanic Villa, 13 Botanic Rd, Glasnevin, **T** 01 830 2180, **F** 01 830 2228, info@family-homes.ie *Map 1, A4, p247* Open all year, this family home provides three en suite doubles and one single.

E Renwell House, 33 Finglas Rd, Glasnevin, **T** 01 830 2061. *Map 1, A3, p247* Situated on a busy street off Phibsborough Road, Renwell House has car parking and affordable rooms.

South of Dublin

The seasonal appeal of Bray means that some of the town's hotels close up for the winter; in summer, on the other hand, everyone wants a room on Strand Road.

Hotels

A-C Gresham Royal Marine, Marine Rd, Dun Laoghaire, **T** 01 280 1911, **F** 01 280 1089, www.gresham-hotels.com By far the classiest hotel in Dun Laoghaire, this place alone makes an extended visit to the seaside suburb worthwhile. The Victorian building has been open to the public since 1865 and offers stirring views of the harbour and the incoming ferries. Elegant, spacious rooms are housed in the old part of the building and in a newer block, with a supplement for harbour views. The hotel also has a sedate restaurant.

B-C **Portview Hotel**, 6/7 Marine Rd, Dun Laoghaire, **T** 01 280 1663, **F** 01 280 0447, portview@club.ie Close to the harbour, this family-run hotel has around 20 bedrooms (eight en suite) and offers a homely atmosphere, open fires, a reliable restaurant and private parking. Special rates are available for children and senior citizens.

D **Esplanade Hotel**, Strand Rd, Bray, **T** 01 286 2056, **F** 01 286 6496, www.regencyhotels.com On the seafront at Bray, this is an evocative-looking hotel, especially when its handsome Victorian façade is lit up at night. Recently renovated, it includes a modern leisure centre, sauna and gym. Check out the website for special deals and discounts. Closed over Christmas.

D **Royal Hotel**, Main St, Bray, **T** 01 286 2935, **F** 01 286 7373, www.regencyhotels.com Twice the size of the Esplanade, this family-friendly hotel offers free movies, weekend music in the bar and a leisure centre with pool.

E **Strand Hotel**, Strand Rd, Bray, **T** 01 286 2327.   Another Victorian-era edifice with some appealing period details, including an interior arch. Open June to September only.

B&Bs

D-E **Ophira**, 10 Corrig Ave, Dun Laoghaire, **T/F** 01 280 099, johnandcathy@ophira.ie There are five guest rooms, four en suite, at this pretty Victorian house in the centre of Dun Laoghaire, plus secure car parking and a TV lounge. Child and senior citizen reductions. No smoking.

E Avondale House, 3 Northumberland Ave, Dun Laoghaire, **T** 01 280 9628, **F** 01 280 5764, harraghy@eircom.net Avondale is small, basic and affordable. Located in a quiet side street, it has six rooms with shared bathrooms. Families welcome; reductions for children.

F Sea Breeze House, 1 Marine Terrace, Bray, **T** 01 286 8337. For those arriving by DART, this is the most conveniently located B&B, facing the sea behind the station. Rooms are all en suite. Closed over Christmas period.

Hostels

F Marina House, Old Dunleary Rd, Dun Laoghaire, **T** 01 284 1524. This is Dun Laoghaire's oldest hostel, with dorm beds for €20, family rooms and one private room for €50. Rates include breakfast; other meals are available. There's a laundry for guest use.

G Belgrave Hall, 34 Belgrave Square, Monkstown, **T** 01 284 2106, info@dublinhostel.com Between Blackrock and Dun Laoghaire, Belgrave Hall has dorm beds, private rooms, free parking, a laundry and bikes for hire. Rates include breakfast.

North of Dublin

Hotels

D Deer Park Hotel, Howth, **T** 01 832 2624, **F** 01 839 2405, sales@deerpark.iol.ie Set in a picturesque hillside location with sea views, the Deer Park has numerous facilities including a restaurant, swimming pool, sauna, golf complex and all-weather tennis courts.

D Marine Hotel, Sutton Cross, Howth **T** 01 839 0000, **F** 01 839 0442. A bustling hotel with a good restaurant, heated indoor pool and comfortable rooms. It's located just five-minutes' walk from the DART.

D-E Bracken Court Hotel, Bridge St, Balbriggan, **T** 01 841 3333, www.brackencourt.ie Bracken Court is a new hotel with a good restaurant and bar in the centre of Balbriggan (north of Skerries), close to the suburban rail station.

D-E White Sands Hotel, Coast Rd, Portmarnock, Malahide, **T** 01 846 0003, **F** 01 846 0420, sandshotel@eircom.net This modern, efficient hotel is right on the seashore with stunning views over Howth and Ireland's Eye. The big bedrooms are comfortable and sunny, a good breakfast is served each morning and the lobby area overlooks an excellent sandy beach. There are coastal walks in both directions, golf links nearby, and a bus journey or brisk walk will take you to the DART at Malahide.

Guesthouses

B-C King Sitric Restaurant and Accommodation, East Pier, Howth, **T** 01 832 5235, **F** 01 839 2442, info@kingsitric.ie Above the famous, eponymous restaurant (p146) is a small guesthouse with eight rooms. It's closed at Christmas and for the last two weeks of January, but at other times of year makes a good alternative to the city centre, particularly if peace and quiet are high on your agenda.

D Redbank Guesthouse, Church St, Skerries, **T** 01 849 0439, **F** 01 849 1598, www.redbank.ie/guesthouse Attached to the well-known Redbank restaurant (p146), this comfortable, friendly guesthouse offers sunny bedrooms, a sitting room, courtyard garden and excellent breakfasts – try the locally smoked salmon and scrambled eggs. It's a great out-of-town place to stay if you don't fancy the weekend furore of the city. The owners of Redbank regularly arrange golfing, fishing, walking and sailing trips in the area for guests.

D Redbank Lodge, 12 Convent Lane, Skerries, **T** 01 849 0439, **F** 01 849 1598, www.redbank.ie/lodge Owned by the same family as Redbank Guesthouse, this is a smaller, more intimate alternative, located in a nearby side street. Breakfast is in the main building, but there's a huge lounge area and a pretty garden for guests to enjoy here.

B&Bs

E Gleann na Smol, Kitty Rickard, Nashville Rd, Howth, **T** 01 832 2936, **F** 01 832 0516, rickards@indigo.ie Close to the DART, this is a modern two-storey house set in its own garden with parking for guests. It's a family-friendly B&B, with reduced rates for children. The four en suite rooms have TVs and tea- and coffee-making facilities.

E Malting House Inn, Holmpatrick, Skerries, **T** 01 849 1075. Accommodation is offered in a pretty, old, stone-built pub close to the Skerries Mills complex. Rates do not include breakfast.

E O'Leary's Thatched Cottage, 39 The Square, Skerries, **F** 01 849 3029, olearysthatchedcottage@oceanfree.net Right in the centre of Skerries, this place has a thatched roof, garden, en suite no-smoking bedrooms and a sauna for guest use. The rooms all have TV and tea-and coffee-making facilities. Extras include a babysitting service and collection from Dublin airport. Guide-dog friendly.

Until the 1990s dining in Dublin was a rather lack-lustre experience: a meal out meant a piece of steak accompanied by a crescent-shaped dish of overcooked vegetables and three kinds of potato. Nowadays, though, the city has everything to offer the gourmet visitor, from trendy tapas bars serving up a little of what you fancy to Michelin-starred restaurants offering more courses than you can shake a menu at. The crescent-shaped dishes are still in evidence, but now the veg is delicately steamed and infinitely more edible.

Fresh seafood is often the highlight of a Dublin menu, with locally sourced Irish beef and lamb providing a treat for carnivores. Dedicated veggie eateries are thin on the ground, but with a bit of planning non-meat-eaters can avoid the ubiquitous vegetable lasagne. The city's ethnic restaurants are a particularly good choice for both vegetarians and their carnivore friends: Chinese and Indian cuisines are well represented, while Southeast Asian food (especially Thai) and Japanese noodles are both becoming increasingly popular.

€ Eating codes

Price

€€€   €36 and over

€€   €19-35

€   €18 and under

Prices refer to the cost of a three-course meal, excluding drinks, for one person.

Temple Bar has a cornucopia of moderately priced eateries, with Italian and traditional Irish restaurants making a particularly strong showing. You'll find plenty of upmarket places in the area around Grafton Street. Restaurants are thinner on the ground north of the river, but those that exist usually have a well-established, reliable reputation. Beyond the city centre is a clutch of individual, independent venues that are worth the bus, DART or cab ride out of town.

Grafton Street and around

Restaurants

€€€ **The Commons**, Newman House, 85-6 St Stephen's Green, **T** 01 475 2597. *Mon-Fri 1230-1415 and 1900-2215, Sat 1230-1415. Map 2, E7, p249* Located downstairs in the attractive old Jesuit university building, The Commons serves a sophisticated combination of classical and nouvelle Irish cuisine surrounded by a collection of James Joyce-inspired paintings. The restaurant is open for a pricey lunch, when men in suits predominate, and for dinner, when less formal attire fills the room. On summer evenings, start off with a pre-dinner drink on the terrace, overlooking the secret world of the Iveagh Gardens.

€€€ **Plurabelle**, Conrad Hotel, Earlsfort Terrace, **T** 01 602 8900. *Daily 0700-2300. Map 2, F8, p249* This successful, busy, brasserie-style restaurant makes a great job of providing Mediterranean/modern Irish fare in appealing surroundings. Tables, clad in pretty white cloths, are comfortably far apart, there's an amazing triptych of old Dublin on one of the walls, the silver-service waiters are friendly without being unctuous and there's no taped music in the background. Come here to enjoy the great early-bird menu before an event at the Concert Hall over the road or while away a whole evening over the stylish dinner menu (€45 for three courses). There's also a very popular buffet-style lunch on Sundays for around €35. Vegetarians need have no fear.

€€€ **Rubicon**, 6 Merrion Row, **T** 01 676 5955. *Mon-Sat 1230-1430 and 1730- 2230, Sun 1730-2230. Map 2, D8, p249* Furiously busy at lunchtime with suits frittering away their expense accounts, this place transforms radically in the evening into a quiet, reflective, romantic spot. The restaurant spreads over two floors with open fires in the basement and muted, modern decor throughout. The subtle fusion menu incorporates the best Irish cheeses, lots of seafood and some good options for vegetarians.

€€ **Aya**, 48 Clarendon St, **T** 01 677 1544. *Mon-Fri 0800-2300, Sat 1000-2300, Sun 1100-2200. Map 2, B7, p249* Dublin's only conveyor-belt Japanese sushi bar offers different menus for breakfast, lunch and dinner, plus other tables for regular dining. The set dinner at €30 is a peculiar mixture of Irish and Japanese dishes, including surf and turf tempura and chocolate cake. An early-bird menu is offered from Monday to Saturday, with five courses and a drink for €21.

€€ **Il Posto**, 10 St Stephen's Green, **T** 01 679 4769. *Mon-Sat 1200-1500, 1800-2300, Sun 1800-2330. Map 2, D8, p249* This is a little gem in the heart of business-lunch Dublin. Located in an

★ **Restaurants for special occasions**

Best

- The Commons, p127
- Tea Room, p133
- Ernie's, p138
- Le Panto, p138
- Halo, p141

easy-to-miss basement, it's about as genuinely Italian as you could find in Dublin. Bare floors, washed-out Mediterranean paintwork and Italian music provide the setting for a mix of traditional and modern food, accompanied by a great wine list. Vegetarians will enjoy the food here if they aren't too choosy. Bear in mind that the à la carte menu is right at the top end of this price range and you're likely to notch up a pretty hefty bill if you have expensive tastes.

€€ **Jaipur** , 41 South Great George's St, **T** 01 677 0999. *Daily 1230-1530 and 1800-2400. Map 2, B6, p248* The decor at Jaipur is refreshingly untypical of your average Indian restaurant – all pale wood, postmodern furniture and mood lighting – and the food is a far cry from typical Indian restaurant fare. Vegetarian options, in particular, are the stuff of dreams.

€€ **Juice**, 73-8 South Great George's St, **T** 01 475 7856. *Daily 1100-2300. Map 2, B6, p248* Juice is a very cool place to consume strange macrobiotic drinks and standard vegetarian fare. There are inexpensive set lunches and a good early-bird menu. Regular customers rave about the veggie burgers.

€€ **Little Caesar**, 5 Chatham House, Balfe St, **T** 01 671 8714. *Daily 1230-0030. Map 2, C7, p249* A Dublin institution that has been operating on this spot for almost 15 years – a very long time in the life of the city's restaurants. Judging by the queues outside,

★ **Cheap eats**

Best

- Govinda's, p131
- Steps of Rome, p131
- Epicurean Food Hall, p142
- Soup Dragon, p143
- Beshoff's, p143

Little Caesar hasn't lost its touch either, serving pizzas, pastas and a few old favourites such as *pollo al fredo* and *bistecca alla griglia*; main courses cost from €13-18.

€€ **Rajdoot**, 26-8 Clarendon St, **T** 01 679 4274. *Daily 1215-1430 and 1800-2300. Map 2, C7, p249* This excellent Indian restaurant provides all the elements of a memorable evening, from elaborate wall hangings to unintrusive background music. Guests relax in a spacious seating area to pick out their meal in consultation with the courteous staff. Nibble on toasted chickpeas while you wait for your order and then tuck into huge, tasty, subtle dishes, including a relatively vast choice for vegetarians. There is no hassle here, no second sittings, just calm and careful service.

€ **Cornucopia**, 19 Wicklow St, **T** 01 677 7583. *Mon-Wed, Fri and Sat 1730-2000, Thu 0530-2100. Map 2, B7, p249* This wholefood vegetarian restaurant is a cut above the sandals-and-dreadlocks image of many similar venues. Breakfast ranges from boxty to granola, French toast and vegetarian fry-ups; lunch and dinner specials are posted up on blackboards. Expect quiche, unusual salads, rice and stews. The drinks list includes wheatgrass options.

€ **Good World Restaurant**, 18, South Great George's St, **T** 01 677 5373. *Daily 1230-0300. Map 2, B6, p248* This place stays open late and so gets lots of custom when the pubs turn out. During the day it is famous for its dim sum and, encouragingly, attracts a fair portion of Chinese customers.

€ **Govinda's**, 4 Aungier St, **T** 01 475 0309. *Mon-Sat 1200-2100. Map 2, C6, p248* Very inexpensive vegetarian food is served here by the Hare Krishna movement. Good lunch specials and breakfasts are available.

€ **Steps of Rome**, Chatham Court, Chatham St, **T** 01 670 5630. *Mon-Thu 1000-2400, Fri-Sat 1000-0100. Map 2, C7, p249* This tiny place is very popular, with crowds often gathering outside to tuck into the takeaway pizzas.

Bars and cafés

Bewley's, Grafton St, **T** 01 677 6761. *Daily 0730-2300. Map 2, C7, p249* There are several branches of Bewley's around the city, but this is the prettiest with stained-glass windows by Harry Clarke. Open for coffee, tea, sandwiches, cakes and more substantial meals, this Dublin landmark can become crowded to the point of panic at lunch and tea, but is more congenial at other times.

Café Bar Deli, 12-13 South Gt George's St, **T** 01 677 1646. *Mon-Thu 1230-2300, Fri and Sat 1230-2400, Sun 1400-2200. Map 2, B6, p248* A former branch of Bewley's Tea Rooms is now a trendy venue serving pastas, salads and pizzas in a very attractive setting. It morphs into a fashionable night spot in the evenings.

Café en Seine, 39/40 Dawson St, **T** 01 677 4567. *Food served Mon-Fri 1200-1500, longer hours on Sat and Sun. Map 2, C8, p249* Be prepared to be gobsmacked: this place is simply spectacular. Before you settle down for food or drink, wander round and admire an over-the-top version of art deco France. Lunch and brunch dishes are more than just snacks and all cost less than a

Time for tea
Traditional food and old-fashioned service are always on the menu at Bewley's.

tenner. Try toasted brioche (the most Francophile item on the menu) or tagliatelle with spinach, cherry tomatoes and pesto, washed down with a margarita or a mai tai. Very, very popular.

Doheny and Nesbitt, 5 Baggot St Lower, **T** 01 676 2945. *Lunch served daily 1200-1500, sandwiches only in the evening. Map 2, D10, p249* Pop into Nesbitt's, as locals call it, to admire the gorgeously authentic Victorian interiors, to listen to the latest Dublin gossip and to feast on the really good pub food: baked potatoes, chilli, paninis, hot beef rolls and BLTs, all tarted up with lots of good pickles and relishes. Finish off the meal with yummy apple pie and coffee.

Havana Tapas Bar, 3 Camden Market, **T** 01 478 0046. *Mon-Thu 1200-2300, Fri and Sat 1200-late. Lunch specials served 1200-1600 Map 2, F5, p248* This modern, bright and stylish place serves little

★ **Best** **Late-night food joints**

- Jaipur, p129
- Little Caesar's, p129
- Good World Restaurant, p130
- Steps of Rome, p131
- Botticelli, p135

dishes that are perfect for grazing – *chorizo frito*, hummus and tortillas, *jamon serrano*, paella – washed down with wine, beer or designer coffee. All dishes are around €7 and there's plenty for vegetarians. Go on Saturday nights for salsa dancing.

Temple Bar and around

Restaurants

€€€ **Les Frères Jacques**, 74 Dame St, **T** 01 679 4555. *Mon-Thu 1230-1400 and 1930-2230, Fri 1230-1430 and 1930-2300, Sat 1930-2300. Map 3, D4, p250* Les Frères Jacques is a French restaurant specializing in classic seafood dishes, but also offering some meat options such as lamb with plum and ginger sauce. The wine list is mostly French. No surprises.

€€€ **Tea Room**, The Clarence, 6-8 Wellington Quay, **T** 01 670 7766. *Daily 1230-1430 and 1830-2230. Map 3, C4, p250* Modern Irish cuisine is served in hushed, elegant surroundings. The simple table decorations, restrained menu and subtle service provide a serene setting for exciting and imaginative cooking. If you're a fan of modern Irish food and can only fork out for one good meal, make it here.

Eating Irish

The traditional food of Ireland is essentially home cooking, based on what the land and the sea could provide. Classic Irish dishes are still readily available in modern Ireland and are well worth trying. Irish stew is familiar to many visitors, but you should also look out for Irish breads such as soda farls, made with wheat flour and leavened with baking soda, or barmbrack, more of a cake than a bread, traditionally produced at Hallowe'en and filled with little tokens that tell the family's fortune.

There isn't room here to describe all the things Irish people do with potatoes, but you should make a point of trying boxty, a mixture of flour, potatoes and buttermilk that's fried into little cakes. (Nowadays they are usually filled with meat.) Another favourite is champ, mashed potato mixed with cooked scallions and melted butter to form the perfect comfort food. At Hallowe'en the speciality is colcannon, which is similar to champ but with cabbage and leeks added to the mix.

In rural Ireland the family pig would traditionally have been slaughtered and salted for the winter to form the basis of that most traditional of Irish workaday meals: bacon and cabbage. A joint of pork is cooked in a pot with cabbage, allowing the two ingredients to absorb one another's essential flavours. They are then served with boiled potatoes in their skins and mustard sauce.

At its best, modern Irish cooking takes all these old favourites and integrates them with the flavours of world cuisine. Champ may be mixed with Thai-style vegetables, while fish caught in Irish waters is served with a Chinese soy and ginger sauce. The capital has some of the most innovative modern Irish restaurants in the country: try the Tea Room at the Clarence, Halo at the Morrison Hotel or Chapter One in Parnell Square.

€€ **Botticelli** , 3 Temple Bar, **T** 01 672 7289. *Daily 1000-2400.*
Map 3, C6, p250 This cosy, tiny place does reasonably priced pizzas
and pasta, some interesting fish and chicken dishes, and tempting
desserts. Ask for a seat overlooking the river, but bear in mind that
this place is very popular. House wine is €16 and the decent
lunchtime menu costs from €8.80 for three courses.

€€ **Eden**, Meeting House Sq, **T** 01 670 5372. *Mon-Fri 1230-1500
and 1800-2230, Sat 1900-2300. Map 3, D4, p250* A Temple Bar
survivor. You know this place is good because it has continued to
thrive long after the herds of chattering classes have moved on to
the next new beech-and-steel, lifestyle restaurant. Good modern
Irish food is served in a stylish context, with seating outside in the
square for long summer afternoons spent people-watching.

€€ **Eliza Blue's**, 23 Wellington Quay, **T** 01 671 9114. *Mon-Fri
0730-1500 and 1700-2300, Sat and Sun 0800-1600 and 1700-2300.
Map 3, C5, p250* Smart, modern decor incorporates polished
wooden tables by the riverside and floor-to-ceiling windows. The
modern European cuisine focuses on seafood, but there are good
meat and vegetarian choices too, including decent lunch specials
for around €8. Live jazz is performed on Monday nights from 2000.

€€ **Fitzer's**, Temple Bar Sq, **T** 01 679 0440. *Daily 1200-2300.
Map 3, C6, p250* Fitzer's has become a Dublin institution, with
branches all around the city. The Temple Bar restaurant is especially
laid back: jazz accompanies the trendy European-style food, which
runs to steaks, burgers and more sophisticated fare.

€€ **Gallagher's Boxty House**, 20-21 Temple Bar, **T** 01 677
2762. *Mon-Fri 1000-2300, Sat 1000-2300, Sun 1100-2200 Map 3,
C7, p250* The eponymous potato-filled pancakes are served in a
simple, country kitchen-style setting. Gallagher's is always popular
and always full.

€€ **Monty's of Kathmandu**, 28 Eustace St, **T** 01 670 4911. *Mon-Sat 1200-1430 and 1800-2330, Sun 1100-2330. Map 3, D5, p250* Great, inexpensive, authentic Nepalese food is on offer at this unpretentious two-floor restaurant, which is full every night and at lunchtime too. The single set menu is accompanied by Monty's own-brewed beer – an Irish bottled lager, with a picture of Lord Shiva on the label. Come early if you want to get a seat, or, better still, make a reservation.

€€ **Nico's**, 53 Dame St, **T** 01 677 3062. *Mon-Fri 1230-1430 and 1800-2400. Map 3, D5, p250* Ask anyone involved in the food business in Dublin where they like to eat and this place usually crops up in the conversation. Nico's unfailing popularity is due to a winning formula of good, traditional Italian food, white tablecloths, Chianti bottles and bustling waiters. Main courses cost from around €16.

€€ **Oliver St John Gogarty**, 58/9 Fleet St, **T** 01 671 1822. *Mon-Sat 1200-2300, Sun 1600-2300. Map 3, C7, p250* This popular pub (p153) serves traditional Irish food in its lively, old-fashioned upstairs restaurant. The best starter by a mile is the vast pot of mussels cooked in wine and Bailey's sauce. Main courses are served with colcannon and there's usually a vegetarian choice. Taped Irish music plays in the background and you can enjoy live music downstairs after your meal. Reservations are always necessary, so come early in the evening to guarantee a table. There is a minimum charge of €17 per person.

Bars and cafés

Central Percs, 10 East Essex St, **T** 01 670 4193. *Mon-Sat 1000-2000. Map 3, C4, p250* Tasty filled baguettes and sandwiches are the order of the day at this quiet, tiny place with a loyal local clientele.

Best

★ **Veggie venues**

- Jaipur, p129
- Juice , p129
- Rajdoot, p130
- Cornucopia, p130
- Monty's of Kathmandu, p136

Freedom Café, Fleet St. *Mon-Sat 0930-2000. Map 3, B8, p250* In among the selection of Amnesty posters, free-trade chocolate bars, bits of ethnic pottery, arty calendars and birthday cards is a neat if tightly-spaced cyber café selling baguettes, ciabatta sandwiches, cakes and the like for €4 or less.

The Liberties and west

Restaurants

€€ **Brazen Head**, 20 Bridge St Lower, **T** 01 679 5168. *Daily 1030-0030. Map 2, A2, p248* Dublin's oldest pub (p155) has a first-floor restaurant with an authentic Victorian feel thanks to its huge dresser, piano and stucco ceilings. The interesting menu combines Californian cuisine with modern Irish cooking served in hearty helpings and includes some decent vegetarian choices. Downstairs is a carvery serving lunch and hot specials. Reservations are usually essential upstairs. There's often live music in the bar.

€€ **Old Dublin Restaurant**, 91 Francis St, **T** 01 454 2028. *Mon-Sat 1230-1430 and 1730-2230, Sun 1730-2230. Map 2, C3, p248* This unusual restaurant is not easy to pigeonhole. Three rooms in a former tenement block have been converted into a relaxed, living room-style eatery that has seasoned with age.

The delightful food is influenced by Scandinavian and Russian cuisine and the wine list is above average. Come for the early evening set dinner from 1830 to 1930.

O'Shea's Merchant, 12 Bridge St Lower, **T** 01 679 3797. *Sun-Wed 1030-2400, Thu-Sat 1030-0230. Map 2, A3, p248* This old-fashioned spot is nothing special as a pub, but its bar food (served until 1800) is good, and includes Irish lunch specials. The huge floor space gets cleared later in the evening for set dancing (p164), with trad music from 2130 till closing.

Ballsbridge and south

Restaurants

€€€ **Ernie's**, Mulberry Gardens, Donnybrook, **T** 01 269 3300. *Tue-Fri 1230-1400 and 1930-2230, Sat 1930-2230.* Off the tourist trail but well worth the bus ride, Ernie's promises impeccable service without servility from dinner-jacketed waiters and a fantastic set dinner menu. On arrival a miniature garden with a pear tree is the first distraction, and then comes a veritable art gallery of original paintings adorning the dining room walls (check out John Doherty's scenes of Castletownbere and Connemara). To reach this local gem, take bus no 46 from Fleet Street or Ballsbridge, or bus no 10 from O'Connell Street or Kildare Street, and ask to be dropped off at Kiely's Pub in Donnybrook. Ernie's is at the end of the lane that runs down the side of the fish-and-chip shop.

€€€ **Le Panto**, Radisson SAS Hotel, Pembroke Rd, **T** 01 660 5000. *Mon-Sat 1230-1400 and 1900-2230, Sun 1230-1400 and 1800-2200. Map 4, C2, p251* Set in the illustrious surroundings of the former private library of Viscount Hugh Gough, who served at the battle of Waterloo, Le Panto boasts a big open fire, lots of space and lovely views over the gardens. The food is haute cuisine served in Irish portions.

€€€ **Raglan's**, Jury's Hotel, Pembroke Rd, **T** 01 660 5000. *Mon-Sat 1215-1400 and 1815-2215, Sun 1230-1400 and 1815-2100. Map 4, C3, p251* Style and amiability have no trouble mixing in this reassuringly Irish restaurant. Soft carpeting, white linen and a pianist playing Yeats songs in the background all contribute to the comforting, sedate atmosphere. The traditional Irish food (lamb, Dover sole) is jazzed up with contemporary sauces, and a spiky Thai curry makes a welcome change from the usual vegetarian option. Parsimonious menu, generous wine list.

€€€ **Roly's**, 7 Ballsbridge Terr, **T** 01 668 2611. *Daily 1200-1445 and 1800-2130. Map 4, E4, p251* Fearfully crowded at all times, Roly's is a Dublin legend, serving reliable Irish favourites tarted up with fashionable accoutrements: chicken stuffed with salmon and Neuberg sauce; fish and chips in beer batter with mushy peas; roast cod with black olive mash and pesto dressing. Ring well in advance to secure a table.

€€ **Baan Thai**, 16 Merrion Rd, **T** 01 660 8833. *Mon and Tue 1800-2300, Wed-Fri 1230-1430 and 1800-2300, Sat 1800-2330. Map 4, E4, p251* The interior of this well established Thai place owes more to Dublin 4 than it does to Koh Samui. Authentic Thai dishes are served in European style as appetisers and there are good business lunch offers for around €8. Vegetarians might have a little trouble, though.

€€ **O'Connell's**, Bewley's Hotel, Merrion Rd, **T** 01 647 3400. *Mon-Sat 1230-1430 and 1830-2230, Sun 1230-1500 and 1800-2130. Map 4, F6, p251* Situated alongside but independent of the hotel, this is an excellent bistro-style restaurant whose interior is dominated by a giant wood-burning stove for making pizzas. It's very popular, especially at lunchtime when the dining choices range from a salad bar to a full three-course meal. The early evening menu, served between 1800 and 1900, is particularly good value, while the full dinner menu offers traditional fare such as loin of pork with cabbage and shallots, and steak with peppercorn sauce. Round off your meal with the neat sample dish of several tiny desserts.

Bars and cafés

Searson's, Baggot St Upper, **T** 01 660 0330. *Sun-Thu 1100-2330, Fri and Sat 1100-0100. Map 2, F12, p249* This huge Victorian pub has been recently renovated. It serves loads of pub food, a carvery lunch as well as an evening menu till 2000.

Café Java, 145 Leeson St Upper, **T** 01 660 0675. *Mon -Fri 0715-1700, Sat 0800-1700, Sun 1100-1700. Map 2, G10, p249* Designer coffees, bagels, wraps and more.

O'Connell St and around

Restaurants

€€€ **Chapter One**, 18-19 Parnell Sq, **T** 01 873 2266. *Tue-Fri 1230-1430 and 1800-2300, Sat 1800-2300. Map 2, E6, p252* Chapter One serves the best food north of the Liffey and has a claim to be considered one of the best restaurants in the city. Organic pork, spicy duck and roast venison are among the delights on the menu and are served in the basement of an elegant Georgian house. If you're attending a performance at the Gate, make the most of the good-value theatre menu at around €30 for three courses.

€€€ **Halo**, Morrison Hotel, Ormond Quay, **T** 01 887 2421.
Daily 0700-1030, 1230-1415 and 1900-2200. *Map 3, B4, p250*
A huge, free-standing black slab, large mirrors and lamp shades
that resemble one of the Wright brothers' flying machines form the
monumental backdrop to this chic restaurant. No one over the age
of 30 seems to venture in here. Munch on Guinness-and-treacle
bread while you choose from a menu of stylish fusion dishes.
Eclectic starters include tour-de-force blinis with smoked tuna,
scallops, caviar and wasabi crème fraiche.

€€€ **23 at the Gresham**, Gresham Hotel, O'Connell St, **T** 01
817 6116. *Mon-Sat 0730-1000, 1200-1430 and 1730-2230.* *Map 5,
F7, p253* Austere table settings, black floors and minimalist wall
decorations combine to create an ultra-cool interior that's in stark
contrast to the Gresham's predominant style (which is rather like
Titanic just before it sank). As a place to eat modern Irish cuisine,
however, 23 is gaining an enviable reputation. The lunch/early
evening menu is good value at three courses for €23.

€€ **Café Royale**, Royal Dublin Hotel, O'Connell St, **T** 01 873
3666. *Daily 1230-1430 and 1800-2230.* *Map 5, F7, p253* Adjoining
the hotel bar is a brasserie-style restaurant that's usually busy but
never frantic. Dubliners flock here for decently priced meals and
the assurance that nothing scandalously minimalist will appear on
the plate. Hearty main courses are meat-based – steak, Irish lamb
with vegetable stew, duck – with a couple of fish dishes thrown in
for good measure. Wannabe sophisticates wouldn't set foot in the
place, but it's mercifully free of mobile phones and no one will
hurry you out once you've finished your meal.

€€ **Il Vignardo**, Hotel Isaac's, Store St, **T** 01 855 6215. *Map 5,
G9, p253* A pizza-based menu is served in a cellar-like vault that
was once part of a wine warehouse. The surroundings are
enlivened, if that's the right word, by florally decorated columns.

★ **Picnic spots**

Best

- Iveagh Gardens, p45
- Custom House Quay, p76
- Phoenix Park, p80
- Howth Head, p98
- Red Island, Skerries, p100

€€ **101 Talbot**, 100-102 Talbot St, **T** 01 874 501. *Tue-Sat 1700-2300. Map 5, G8, p253* The reviews posted outside 101 Talbot confirm that there is good food to be enjoyed inside this northside restaurant. Modern Irish cuisine with a Mediterranean inflection is served at reasonable prices. Vegetarians will especially enjoy this place.

€ **Epicurean Food Hall**, Liffey St Lower. *Mon-Sat 0900-1930. Map 5, H6, p252* This food hall is full of stalls selling all manner of exotic cooked food, with tables provided in a central area. It gets seriously crowded during the day when you'll be lucky to find a seat, but for around €7 for loads of tasty grub maybe it's worth the scrum. Many stalls close before 1930.

€ **Flanagan's**, 61 O'Connell St, **T** 01 873 1388. *Daily 1200-2300. Map 5, G7, p253* Flanagan's serves unchallenging food – pizzas, steaks and some vegetarian choices – at very reasonable prices. The three-course dinner costs under €15 and you can tuck into soup, garlic bread and pizza for under €10.

€ **The Italian Connection**, 95 Talbot St, **T** 01 878 7125. *Daily 0800-2200. Map 5, G8, p253* Pizzas take pride of place on the menu at this tiny, pleasant restaurant, with trompe l'oeil paintings on the walls and simple place settings.

€ **Soup Dragon**, 168 Capel St, **T** 01 872 3277. *Mon-Fri 0800-1730, Sat 1100-1700. Map 5, H5, p252* Restaurants don't come much smaller than this place. A few stools cluster around a bar where dreamy soups are served. Soup plus bread costs around €7. Takeaway service.

Bars and cafés

Beshoff's, 16 O'Connell St, **T** 01 872 4400. *Mon-Wed 1100-2100, Thu-Sat 1100- 2300. Map 5, G7, p253* One of a chain of great fish-and-chip caffs, Beshoff's has a pleasantly scruffy Edwardian interior that provides a perfect setting in which to dig into a mound of authentic grub. The first Beshoff's was opened by Ivan Iylanovich, a survivor of the 1905 mutiny aboard the battleship *Potemkin*.

Kudos, Clarion Hotel, Excise Walk, **T** 01 433 8844. *Daily 1200-2030. Map 3, B4, p250* Three wok stations conjure up some innovative and tasty combinations of European and Asian cuisine for very decent prices in this new, laid-back bar in the riverside Clarion Hotel (p114).

Pravda , 35 Liffey St Lower, **T** 01 874 0076. *Mon-Wed 1200-2330, Thu 1100-0030, Fri and Sat 1100-0200, Sun 1100-2300. Map 3, A6, p250* A Russian-themed café bar that does wraps and baguettes, though people come to Pravda to drink rather than eat.

Zanzibar, 36 Ormond Quay Lower, **T** 01 878 7212. *Daily 1700-0230. Map 3, B3, p250* This vast, youthful place reputedly cost squillions to build and is heavily themed with palm trees and Middle Eastern décor. The bar food is substantial, ranging from nachos to chicken and steak dishes and even a vegetarian effort. If you don't like crowds of drunken youth, don't visit: although Zanzibar holds about 1,500, there's usually a queue at weekends.

From Smithfield to the Phoenix Park

Restaurants

€€ **Kelly and Ping**, Smithfield Village, **T** 01 817 3840. *Mon-Fri 1100-2300, Sat 1700-2300, Sun 1100-1800.* *Map 5, H2, p252* This fusion eatery serves lots of lemon grass and coconut milk but also Malay, Chinese and Japanese classics. The jury's still out on the quality of the food, but there's a pleasant-enough cocktail bar (happy hour 1700-2000), with huge painted murals and buddhas.

€€ **Nancy Hands**, 30 Parkgate St, **T** 01 677 0177. *Mon-Fri 1200-1500 and 1800-2200, Sat 1200-1630 and1800-2230, Sun 1800-2200.* *Map 6, F9, p255* This Irish theme pub (p157) gets great reviews for its food: a carvery lunch, bar food and a more formal dinner menu that mixes Asian and modern Irish elements.

€€ **Ryan's of Parkgate Street**, 28 Parkgate St, **T** 01 671 9352. *Thu-Sat 1900-2200.* *Map 6, F9, p255* Above the impressive, century-old bar (p158) is an equally magnificent restaurant with marble fireplaces and a Victorian living room feel. Home-style food is served in hearty portions, and is a cut above usual pub grub.

South of Dublin

Restaurants

€€€ **Brasserie na Mara**, 1 Harbour Rd, Dun Laoghaire, **T** 01 280 6767. *Mon-Fri 1230-1430 and1830- 2230, Sat 1830-2230.* The mostly seafood menu at this very long-established restaurant is innovative and fashionable. Enjoy casual dining on bare beech tables in an elegant room.

€€ **Caviston's**, 59 Glasthule Rd, Sandycove, Dun Laoghaire, **T** 01 280 9120. *Tue-Sat 1200-1700.* Caviston's is a small seafood restaurant offering really fresh fish dishes. There are three lunch sittings at this very popular place, so choose your favoured time when booking.

€€ **Duzy's** , 18 Glasthule Rd, Dun Laoghaire, **T** 01 230 0210. *Mon-Thu 1230-1430 and 1730-2200, Fri 1230-1430 and 1730-2230, Sat 1730-2230, Sun 1230-1500 and 1800-2100.* Duzy's is a relaxed venue with wooden tables, comfy chesterfields and a cosy bar. The health-conscious menu is based around modern Irish and Mediterranean cuisine, with Asian elements for interest. All dishes are served with a comforting portion of champ and vegetarians are well provided for. An early-bird menu (€18.50) is served between 1530 and 1900.

€€ **Nosh**, 111 Coliemore Rd, Dalkey, **T** 01 284 0666. *Tue-Sun 1200-1600 and 1800-late.* The proud recipient of numerous rave reviews, this trendy Dalkey eatery serves good no-nonsense food – fish and chips, apple crumble – alongside more exotic offerings such as Thai seafood curry or linguine with lobster and crab in amaretto sauce. Main courses are about €18.

€€ **Powerscourt Room**, Royal Marine Hotel, Dun Laoghaire, **T** 01 280 1911. *Sun-Fri 1230-1430 and 1730-2130, Sat 1730-2130.* Tasty, if unremarkable, Irish cuisine is served in this big Victorian dining room with white cloths, pleasant service, a relaxed atmosphere and huge bay windows overlooking the harbour. On Sunday, indulge in afternoon tea in the drawing room.

€€ **The Queen's/Vico**, Castle St, Dalkey, **T** 01 285 4569. *Daily 1230-1400 and 1800-2145.* On the ground floor, The Queen's serves some very good bar food, while upstairs is the more formal Vico restaurant.

Bars and cafés

Scott's Café, 17 George St Upper, Dun Laoghaire, **T** 01 280 2657. *Mon-Thu 1200-2300, Fri and Sat 1200-late.* Split between a downstairs café-bar and an upstairs pub, Scott's Café delivers lots of good bar food and music in the evenings.

Kitchen , Old Dunleary Rd, Dun Laoghaire, **T** 01 284 3576. *Daily till 2400.* Handily placed opposite Dun Laoghaire's only hostel, the Kitchen serves mighty good pub food.

North of Dublin

Restaurants

€€€ **King Sitric**, East Pier, Howth, **T** 01 832 5235. *Mon-Fri 1200-1430 and 1830-2300, Sat 1830-2300.* This well-established and utterly reliable seafood restaurant has garnered lots of recommendations and has some stirring sea views. There's a good set lunch on weekdays.

€€€ **Redbank Restaurant**, 7 Church St, Skerries, **T** 01 849 1005. *Mon-Sat 1900-2130, Sun 1230-1530.* If it swims in Dublin Bay, chances are it'll be on the menu at this excellent seafood restaurant set in an old bank building. The chef greets you at the door and there are tasty pre-dinner snacks to whet your appetite while you choose your meal. Dublin Bay prawns are the speciality of the house, served in several different styles: for a starter try the sizzling, garlicky version, which comes noisily to your table wafting heavenly aromas behind it. Meat eaters and vegetarians have good choices, too. Leave room for a pud from the wackily designed dessert trolley.

Pubs, bars and clubs are what Dublin does best. Dedicated venues around the city offer live traditional music and dancing, jazz nights, salsa nights, country nights, quiz nights, sports nights and just plain drinking nights. Café-bars provide snacks and sophistication, while old-fashioned pubs still ooze that inimitable Dublin character that so many visitors come here to experience.

Tourists flock to Temple Bar, where you can choose to party well into the early hours on any night of the week. Elsewhere, the area that really breaks the *craic* barrier is South Great George's Street and Camden Street, which from Thursday to Sunday seem to turn into a huge street party. This is where young Dubliners come to kick-start their weekends, beginning at The Globe, Hogan's or the Bleeding Horse, moving on when the mood takes them to a club on Harcourt Street – depending on the entrance charge, the DJ or the price of Bacardi breezers – before finally slipping home to sleep it off as the street cleaners arrive to clear up the night's excesses.

Dublin clubs go in and out of fashion faster than Superman can change his lycra, so probably the best way of spotting the city's latest happening place is to follow the crowds. Otherwise check out the listings in the *Event Guide* or *In Dublin* (p214) and watch the pub notice boards. A Dub club may be little more than the upstairs or basement room of one of the city's many bars, or it may be a huge, over-designed nightlife venue catering for a specific type of music, or age group or sexual orientation on different nights.

Pubs and bars are open until 2330 during the week, with many having extended opening hours until 0100 or later at the weekend. Clubs stay open later still and charge admission, although some are free early in the evening in order to tempt the punters inside. Admission charges vary according to the day, time, the DJ and the overall popularity of the venue, ranging from around €3 midweek upstairs in The International to €25 in Spirit on a Saturday night.

Note that pubs that serve particularly good food are listed in the Eating and drinking chapter (p125), while those that are renowned for music, dance or comedy are listed in the Arts and entertainment chapter (p159).

Grafton Street and around

Bars and pubs

The Bailey, 2 Duke St, **T** 01 670 4939. *Mon-Sat 1130-2330, Sun 1600-2330. Map 2, B7, p249* This busy office workers' pub serves good food and gets lively in the evenings. Come here to mingle with journalists and arty types, and to sit outside under the gas braziers to watch the street life.

Bleeding Horse, 24 Camden St, **T** 01 475 2706. *Mon-Wed 1200-2400, Thu 1200-0100, Fri and Sat 1200-0200, Sun 1200-2330. Map 2, F6, p248* The Bleeding Horse has big dark timbers, high

19th-century ceilings and a history going back to Cromwell's time, but also floors and floors of fun, a studenty atmosphere and an upstairs restaurant.

Chocolate Bar, Hatch St Upper, **T** 01 478 0166. *Mon-Thu 1700-2330, Fri 1730-0100, Sat 1800-0100, Sun 1800-2330. Map 2, F7, p249* The bar attached to the POD nightclub (p152) is just too trendy for words. It's seriously well designed and attracts a self-consciously gorgeous clientele, with fashion police on the doors to keep it that way.

Davy Byrne's, 21 Duke St, **T** 01 677 5217. *Mon-Wed 1000-2330, Thu-Sat 1000-0030, Sun 1200-2300. Map 2, F7, p249* This place heaves by day and night. Remnants of its famous literary past are still in evidence: sketches by Cecil French Salkheld, an amazing old mirror, but not the gorgonzola sandwiches that Leopold Bloom ate here in *Ulysses* (except on Bloomsday, of course, p176).

The Globe, 11 South Great George's St, **T** 01 671 1220. *Mon-Thu, Sun 1200-2330, Fri- Sat 1100-0130. Map 2, B6, p248* Young, fashionable and crowded, The Globe offers good food and occasional live jazz on Sunday afternoons.

Hogan's, 35 South Great George's St, **T** 01 677 5904. *Mon-Wed 1300-2330, Thu 1300-0030, Fri and Sat 1030-0230, Sun 1500-2330. Map 2, B6, p248* Another hangout for young fashionable types, with a huge airy interior and an eclectic music policy.

The International, 23 Wicklow St, **T** 01 677 9250. *Mon-Wed 1130-2330, Thu-Sat 1130-0030, Sun 1100-2300. Map 2, B7, p249* Arriving at this Victorian pub can be a rather daunting experience, as everybody stops talking to see who's just walked in. Downstairs is a comedy club and upstairs there's live music. It's raucous at times and **attracts** a very young crowd.

Bars and clubs

Best

★ **Unreconstructed Dublin pubs**

- Doheny & Nesbitt, p132
- The International, p150
- Long Hall, p151
- Palace, p153
- Ryan's of Parkgate Street, p158

Long Hall, 51 South Great George's St, **T** 01 475 1590. *Mon-Wed 1100-2330, Thu 1100-0030, Fri 1200-0030, Sat 1030-0030, Sun 1400-2300. Map 2, C6, p248* If you want a genuinely traditional Irish pub with a glorious interior, this is it.

Messrs Maguire, 1-2 Burgh Quay, **T** 01 670 5777. *Daily 1030-0130. Map 5, H8, p253* With a late bar every night, its own micro-brewery, an astonishing bar-food menu, giant TV screens for sports fans and traditional music evenings, Messrs Maguire caters to all comers. There are lots of little nooks and crannies to hang out in and all the requisite faux Victorian wood panelling you could possibly want.

O'Donoghue's, 15 Merrion Row, **T** 01 660 7194. *Mon-Wed 1030-1130, Thu-Sat 1030-0030, Sun 1230-2300. Map 2, D9, p249* An unreconstructed and pleasant old pub, with lots of impromptu music sessions and an unusual mix of tourists and locals.

Clubs

Bojangles, Russell Court Hotel, Harcourt St, **T** 01 478 4066. *Daily 2000-late. €8. Map 2, F6, p248* Frequented by the over-30s, this long-established club beneath the Russell Court Hotel hosts a good salsa night (including lessons) on Thursdays from 2000.

Bars and clubs

★ Cool bars

Best

• Café en Seine, p131
• The Bailey, p149
• Chocolate Bar, p150
• Front Lounge, p153
• Dice Bar, p157

Gaiety, South King St, **T** 01 679 5622. *Fri and Sat 2400-0400. €12. Map 2, C7, p249* This old theatre offers three floors of fun: retro hits in the basement, cartoon- and movie-screenings in the auditorium, live salsa and jazz in the main bar and DJs upstairs.

Mono, 26 Wexford St, **T** 01 475 8555. *Mon-Thu, Sun 1600-0230, Fri and Sat 1600-0300. Free. Map 2, F6, p248* Very young, very studenty and very boozy. There's music in the bar from 2100 till late and big-name DJs from across the water at weekends.

POD/Redbox, Old Harcourt St Station, Harcourt St. **T** 01 478 0225. *Wed-Sun 2300-0300. €13. Map 2, F7, p249* These twin super-clubs are seriously stylish and attract a high proportion of clubbers who have an inflated idea of their own attractiveness. Drinks are cheaper on Wednesdays when a studenty tone prevails.

Spy/Wax, Powerscourt Centre, South William St, **T** 01 677 0014. *Tue-Sat 2100-0300, Sun 2200-0300. Spy free Tue-Thu before 2330, €12 at other times. Wax €12. Map 2, B7, p249* These perennially sophisticated clubs are usually full of cool, rich people eyeing each other up. Sunday is one of Dublin's top gay nights (p201).

Sugar Club, 8 Leeson St Lower, **T** 01 678 7188, www.thesugarclub.com *Wed-Sat 2030-late. €5-15. Map 2, E8, p249* There are DJs on Friday and Saturday nights at this new venue on

Bars and clubs

the site of the old Sugar Company. Cinema screens show old movies for the chill-out crowd, while the sound-proofed cocktail lounge offers an escape from the hubbub.

Temple Bar and around

Bars and pubs

Auld Dubliner, 17 Anglesea St, T 01 677 0527. *Mon-Thu 1030-2330, Fri and Sat 1030-0030, Sun 1230-2300. Map 3, C7, p250* Tuned into the huge tourist trade of Temple Bar, the Auld Dubliner serves up good bar food (including coddle) and live traditional music.

Front Lounge, 33-34 Parliament St, T 01 670 4112. *Mon, Wed, Sun 1200-2330, Tue 1200-2400, Thu-Sat 1200-0130. Map 3, D3, p250* Comfy sofas, clever lighting and an extensive wine list ensure that the Front Lounge remains one of Dublin's most popular bars. Don't come here if you want to have a knees-up.

Octagon Bar, Clarence Hotel, 6-8 Wellington Quay, T 01 670 9000. *Mon-Sat 1000-2300, Sun 1230-2230. Map 3, C4, p250* This is possibly the coolest bar in town, with good cocktails, big sofas and occasional visits from A-list celebs.

Oliver St John Gogarty, 58-59 Fleet St, T 01 677 5213. *Daily 1030-0200. Map 3, C7, p250* Completely tourist oriented but in a good way, this faux trad pub offers great bar food (p136) and live music every afternoon and evening. There are lots of little nooks to sit in, vestiges of old Ireland on the walls and a lively atmosphere.

Palace, 21 Fleet St, T 01 677 9290. *Mon-Wed 1030-2330, Thu-Sat 1030-0030, Sun 1230-2300. Map 3, B8, p250* This is where people who live and work in Temple Bar go for a quiet drink, it's a friendly

old pub that remains totally unfazed by the maelstrom that rages on the streets outside.

Temple Bar, 45 Temple Bar, **T** 01 672 5286. *Mon-Wed 1100-2400, Thu-Sat 1100-0030, Sun 1200-0030. Map 3, C6, p250* The unmissable red exterior lures tourists and locals into this popular pub. It's heaving at all hours, with live traditional music every afternoon. The fun spills out into the beer garden in the summer.

Turk's Head, 27-30 Parliament St, **T** 01 679 9701. *Daily 1630-0200. Map 3, C6, p250* This overpoweringly decorated bar has good bar food and a belly dancer on Tuesdays. Lots of tourists generate a singalong atmosphere that lasts late into the night.

Clubs

The Ballroom, Fitzsimmons Hotel, East Essex St, **T** 01 677 9387. *Daily 2200-02300. €6-7. Map 3, C5, p250* This huge pub basement attracts a largely tourist crowd whose aim is to get very tip friends before staggering back to their hotel room at three morning. Lots of retro faves on the turntable.

Club M, Blooms Hotel, Anglesea St, **T** 01 671 5622. *0230. €7. Map 3, D7, p250* A booze-fuelled, tourist-oriented easy-listening pick-up joint that's enjoyable enough, place that kind of thing.

Temple Bar Music Centre, Curved St, **T** 01 670 9202. *floors, 1030-0230. €13 . Map 3, C6, p250* This huge place is really a venue (p167) but offers club nights after each gig, which are free to those who've attended the live event. Tuesday is salsa night with dance lessons followed by a dedicated club night. For discounted admission, pick up a flyer from the foyer or from the tourist office.

The Liberties and west

Bars and pubs

Brazen Head, 20 Bridge St Lower, **T** 01 679 5168. *Daily 1030-0030. Map 2, A2, p248* Dublin's oldest pub has heaps of atmosphere, a mixed clientele, good food (p137) and trad music.

Molloy's, 13 High St, **T** 01 677 3207. *Opening hours vary. Map 2, B3, p248* This small pub runs a diverse schedule of activities ranging from lesbian nights to singer-songwriter competitions. It's often packed out.

Thomas House, 86 Thomas St, **T** 671 6987. *Mon-Wed 1100-2330, Thu-Sat 1100-0030, Sun 1100-2300. Map 2, B2, p248* Popular with art students, this small, somewhat seedy bar has plenty of ⁺ᵐᵒˢᵖhere and hosts some good club nights.

nell Street and around

⁻⁻ᵖs

9 Abbey St Lower, **T** 01 874 4106. *Mon-Wed ⁻Sat 1130-0030, Sun 1200-2300. Map 5, G8, p253* ⌐tors and back-stage workers from the Abbey ⌐s the street. The walls are covered with pictures ⌐ᵤ performers, who called the place their local.

Parnell Mooney, 72 Parnell St, **T** 01 873 1544. *Map 5, F6, p252* Built in 1868, this place retains much of its Victorian atmosphere and hosts good club nights. You'll often see ashen-faced men here, waiting for news from the Rotunda Hospital across the road.

Patrick Conway's, 70 Parnell St, **T** 01 873 2687. *Mon–Wed, Sun 1000–2330, Thu–Sat 1000–0030. Map 5, F6, p252* First licensed in 1745, this is the oldest pub on the north side. It has a big open-plan bar with lots of space for people-watching, and, like the Parnell Mooney, is often frequented by fledgling fathers celebrating their new status in life. Legend has it that during the bad old days of public life, those infamous brown envelopes changed hands here.

Toddy Bar, Gresham Hotel, O'Connell St, **T** 01 874 688. *Mon–Wed and Sun 1000–2330, Thu–Sat 1000–0030. Map 2, F7, p253* This is a popular meeting place for Dubliners in suits thanks to comfortable seating and over 60 different types of whiskey.

Clubs

Lobo, Morrison Hotel, Ormond Quay, **T** 01 887 2400. *Fri and Sat 2230–0300, €10. Map 3, B4, p250* A cool, beautifully designed place where you might need to book a table. Very chic people come here to chill out and listen to funky jazz sets on Fridays and chart music on Saturdays. Draft beer used to be served, but the pumps spoiled the clean lines of the bar, so now you'll have to make do with cocktails and bottled beer.

Spirit, 57 Middle Abbey St, **T** 01 877 9999, www.spiritdublin.c[...] *Thu–Sat 2200–0300, €25. Map 5, H7, p253* Formerly HQ, this [...] is now a vast, newly reconstructed, overcrowded entertainm[...] complex, with assorted layers of bars, cinema screens, danc[...] a strip joint, a restaurant – yada, yada, yada – all named after different spiritual states.

| The Duke of Wellington got married in St George's Church (now the Temple Theatre) in 1806, although it's rather difficult to imagine him marching down the aisle these days.

Temple Theatre, St George's Church, Temple St, **T** 01 874 5088. *Wed-Sat 2130-0300. €15. Map 5, D7, p253* The nave of this church has been converted into a huge dance floor that jumps to a high-octane party vibe. There's a quieter atmosphere in the crypt.

From Smithfield to the Phoenix Park

Bars and pubs

Chancery Inn, Inns Quay, **T** 01 677 0420. *Mon-Wed, Sun 1000-2300, Thu-Sat 1000-0030. Map 5, H3, p252* An interesting, old-fashioned pub with good live traditional music nightly.

Cobblestone, 77 North King St (entrance on Red Cow Lane), Smithfield, **T** 01 872 1799. *Mon-Wed 1600-2330, Thu-Sat 1600-0030, Sun 1230-2330. Map 5, G2, p252* Surrounded by soon-to-be demolished buildings, the Cobblestone looks as if it has been condemned, but this just makes the surprise of the interior all the more pleasant: a cosy, country-style pub with a great programme of live music (p165), dominated by locals rather than tourists.

Dice Bar, Queen St, **T** 01 872 8622. *Mon-Wed 1030-2330, Thu-Sat 1030-0030, Sun 1030-2300. Map 5, H1, p252* This Manhattan-esque joint in Smithfield comes complete with a bar counter taken from the Delano Beach Hotel in Miami. The cool, bare interior attracts a discerning clientele and there are DJs seven nights a week.

Nancy Hands, 30-32 Parkgate St, **T** 01 677 0177. *Mon-Wed 1230-2330, Thu-Sat 1230-0030, Sun 1230-2300. Map 6, F9, p255* This faux Victorian pub has been assembled piece by reclaimed piece from the remnants of Welsh butchers' shops, Yorkshire churches and Dublin's own Trinity College. It has good food (p144), some pleasant nooks, and, they say, 200 varieties of whiskey.

Step back in time

Despite a rash of designer bars, Dublin still has plenty of local, old-fashioned boozers to discover.

Ryan's, 22 Parkgate St, **T** 01 677 6097. *Mon-Wed 1230-2330, Thu-Sat 1230-0030, Sun 1230-2300. Map 6, F9, p255* This charming old pub looks so authentic that it's hard to believe it wasn't purpose-built as a film set for some American movie about Ireland. In fact, it's as genuine as they come, but if you do get a feeling of déjà vu, it's because Ryan's is regularly used in television programmes and adverts.

Clubs

Voodoo, Arran Quay, **T** 01 874 8050. *Mon-Wed 1100-1230, Thu-Sat 2200-0200, Sun 1200-0100. €8 after 2200. Map 2, A2, p248* This spacious bar has images of the undead lining the walls. It's a drinking den from Monday to Wednesday, with a more clubby vibe predominating from Thursday to Saturday. Be warned: Sunday is Irish country music night.

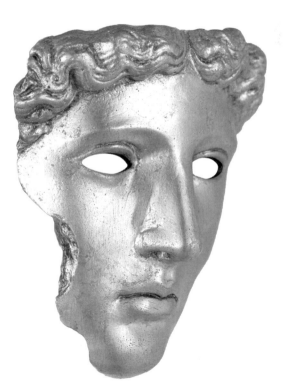

Having gone through the artistic doldrums for a hundred years or so, with talent leaking out of the place as fast as the green card would allow, Dublin in the 21st century once more enjoys a thriving and increasingly international cultural life, with dedicated festivals supporting a vibrant year-round arts scene.

Dublin's renowned theatres offer both international and local productions, while the city's cinemas show all the usual blockbusters plus a welcome sprinkling of arthouse films. Two classical orchestras, an opera company, plus small music groups and choirs all give regular concerts around the city, while innumerable traditional Irish bands perform in Dublin's pubs. Add to this a brand new performance venue, the revival of traditional Irish dancing (once the preserve of ten-year-old girls with fierce braids and fiercer mothers) and the flowering of Irish humour on the stand-up comedy circuit, and you have a recipe for great entertainment in the city.

Cinema

Dublin has a good selection of mainstream multiplexes, both in the city centre and the suburbs. The largest is the nine-screen **UGC** complex in the Parnell Centre at the top of O'Connell Street. For something a little more esoteric, the **Irish Film Centre** in Temple Bar offers a healthy alternative to Hollywood and hosts free outdoor movie screenings in the summer, using one wall of **Meeting House Square** as a huge cinema screen. Look out, too, for the arthouse fare on offer at the **Screen** in D'Olier Street. The **Dublin Film Festival** usually takes place in March or April (p175) and is followed by a **French Film Festival** in November.

Irish Film Centre, 6 Eustace St, Temple Bar, **T** 01 679 3477. *Daily 1330-2130. €5.80 afternoon shows, €6.30 evening shows. Map 3, D5, p250* The centre shows a mixture of independent, foreign and arthouse films as well as documentaries and seasons of a particular director's work. Admission is for members only, but you can buy weekly membership for €1.30, which allows you to buy tickets for yourself and three guests.

Savoy, 6-17 O'Connell St, **T** 01 874 8487. *€6.50 before 1800, €7.50 after 1800. Map 5, F8, p253* The Savoy has five screens showing all the latest blockbusters from Hollywood.

Screen, D'Olier St, **T** 01 672 5500. *€7.50. Map 2, A8, p249* Three screens show a mixture of arthouse and mainstream films daily from1500 to 1930.

UGC Cinemas, Parnell St, **T** 01 872 8444. *€5 before 1800, €6.50 after 1800. Map 5, F5, p252* Catch all the big movies at this nine-screen complex.

On location

While Ireland's film industry has always been a bit short on cash, the country has been an excellent source of actors, directors and movie locations. Dublin, in particular, is a seasoned star of the silver screen. Scenes from *The Italian Job* and the musical *Oliver!* were both filmed inside Kilmainham Gaol, while Trinity College was used in *Educating Rita*. The city's back streets became Limerick for *Angela's Ashes* and a piece of nearby Wicklow mountainside stood in for Scotland in *Braveheart*.

As well as acting as a screen double, the city also stars as itself. The grimier sections of north Dublin went on display both in *My Left Foot*, filmed on location there in 1989, and in Alan Parker's adaptation of Roddy Doyle's novel *The Commitments*, which became a worldwide hit the following year. In 1996 various sites around Dublin were used in the movie *Michael Collins*, and in 1998 John Boorman used the city as a backdrop for *The General,* based on the life of a genuine Dublin crook . More recent Dublin films include *About Adam*, the first Irish production with a bisexual hero, written and directed by Gerald Sternbridge, and *When Brendan met Trudy*, directed by Kieron J Walsh from a screenplay by Roddy Doyle.

Television loves Dublin, too. Strolling around the city you may find yourself an extra in an episode of RTÉ's *Bachelor's Walk*. The British-made soap *Ballykissangel* is filmed just south of Dublin in County Wicklow, and the BBC/RTÉ production *Rebel Heart*, about the years leading up to Home Rule, was partly filmed in Dublin city centre. The Iveagh Gardens, for instance, were used to portray St Stephen's Green during the 1916 Easter Rising, with a notice board at the park entrance to reassure locals that the sounds of gunfire were only blanks fired by actors.

Comedy

Most of the big names in Irish stand-up comedy – and there are several: Ardal O'Hanlon, Tommy Tiernan, Graham Norton, Jason Byrne, Dylan Moran – now work in the UK, but Dublin supports a lively local scene, especially at some of the gay-friendly venues. The majority of Dublin's comedy nights take place in clubs or bars on a weekly basis. For details, consult the Event Guide (p214) or look on notice boards for flyers. The city's most significant comedy venue is **Murphy's Laughter Lounge** on Eden Quay, which is currently closed for rebuilding. Look out for the newly reopened venue in 2004. You should also keep an eye out for one-off comedy nights at GUBU (p201) and the Olympia (p166).

Ha'penny Bridge, 42 Wellington Quay, Temple Bar, **T** 01 677 0616. *Tue-Thu 2130*. €6. *Map 3, B6, p250* This is the place where many big-name comics first cut their teeth. Tuesday night is the 'Battle of the Axe', featuring a variety of amateur acts competing for the Lucky Duck Award, voted for by the audience. All manner of people turn up to try their luck and the audience contributes its fair share of colourful commentary. Wednesday is more traditional organized stand up, while Thursday is improv night, with a team of comics performing sketches based on audience suggestions.

The International, 23 Wicklow St, **T** 01 677 9250. *Mon and Thu 2100*. €7.50. *Map 2, B7, p249* The upstairs bar currently hosts the homeless Murphy's Laughter Lounge on Thursday nights and its own brand of improvisation on Mondays. It has a good atmosphere and probably the best of Dublin's up-and-coming comics in house.

Sugar Club, 8 Leeson St Lower, **T** 01 678 7188. *Thu 2100*. €13. *Map 2, E8, p249* This very fashionable nightclub (p152) offers pre-club stand-up sessions by some well-known Dublin comics.

Dance

You're unlikely to encounter that icon of manufactured Irish culture known to the world at large as 'Riverdance' in Dublin but there are lots of places where you can watch the authentic, less spectacular version. The city is also developing a contemporary dance scene that incorporates Irish traditions of storytelling; look out for performances by the **Irish Modern Dance Theatre**, **T** 01 878 7784, and the **Dance Theatre of Ireland**, **T** 01280 3455, in various venues around the city. Visiting international dance groups often perform in Dublin; consult the Event Guide for details (p214).

Traditional Irish

Arlington Hotel, 23-25 Bachelor's Walk, O'Connell Bridge, **T** 01 804 9100. *Map 5, H7, p253* Live music and dancing are held nightly in the Knightsbridge Bar.

Cultúrlann na hÉireann, 32 Belgrave Sq, Monkstown, **T** 01 280 0295. *Fri 2000 lessons, 2100 dancing. €6.50.* A popular place in the suburbs where locals and visitors can learn set dances accompanied by live ceilidh bands.

O'Shea's Merchant, 12 Bridge St Lower, **T** 01 679 3797. *Daily 2100-0030. Map 2, A2, p248* As soon as the kitchen stops serving (p138), the downstairs bar is cleared for nightly set dancing to live music. Watch or join in.

Taylor's Three Rock, Grange Rd, Rathfarnham, **T** 01 494 2999, www.TaylorsThreeRock.com *Daily dinner 1930, dance show 2115.* Enjoy dinner followed by a show of traditional Irish dancing and singing in a thatched-roof pub, half an hour's drive south of the city centre. Advance booking essential.

Music

Rock, pop and traditional Irish

Dublin is renowned as a musical city, churning pop stars out on to the international stage, while maintaining a lively and varied scene at home. So many venues in Dublin offer live music of one sort or another it would be impossible to list them all here. Besides traditional Irish, there are jazz concerts, tribute bands, visiting megastars and everything in between. You can't go far in this city without tripping over a reference to U2 or hearing the strains of an Irish ballad, but mediocre background music should be avoided if at all possible, unless you're out for a drink with friends and not really fussed about the music. Generally speaking, the more geared towards tourists a place is, the less likely you are to enjoy an authentic cultural experience.

The venues listed below are places where the music comes first. Large-scale rock and pop gigs also take place at the Gaiety (p171), the National Stadium, POD (p152) and the Royal Dublin Showground (p169), while numerous pubs and bars, including Oliver St John Gogarty (p153) and the Brazen Head (p155), host live music of varying style and quality.

Ambassador, Parnell St, **T** 1890 925 100 for credit card bookings. *From €15. Map 5, F6, p252* Dublin's newest and oldest venue, the Ambassador was formerly a cinema and, before that, was the Assembly Rooms of the Rotunda Hospital. It now hosts big-name music concerts with a capacity of 1,200.

Cobblestone, 77 North King St (entrance on Red Cow Lane), Smithfield, **T** 01 872 1799. *Bar music Thu and Fri 1900-0030, Sat 1630-1830 and 1900-0030, Sun 1330, 1700, 2100. Free. First-floor venue Thu-Sat 2030-0030. Admission varies. Map 5, G2, p252*

This Smithfield pub (p157) has a relaxed side bar where dedicated traditional musicians play to appreciative locals without crowds of tourists staring at them. (Bluegrass is performed on Saturday afternoons.) Upstairs is a more serious venue with an eclectic music policy, where the audience are expected to listen carefully rather than talking loudly over the music.

Eamon Doran's, 3A Crown Alley, Temple Bar, **T** 01 679 9114. *Daily 2100-0200. €4-8. Map 3, C6, p250* Good traditional music is performed upstairs every night in summer and on Sundays in winter, with rock gigs on the ground floor.

Harcourt Hotel, 60-61 Harcourt St, **T** 01 478 3677. *Mon-Sat 2130-0030. Free. Map 2, F6, p248* Decent traditional Irish music is performed in the bar of this very tourist-orientated hotel. Jazz and pop acts also make the occasional appearance.

Isaac Butt, Store St, **T** 01 855 5021. *Daily 2030 till late. Map 5, G9, p253* A young, inebriated crowd make the most of live rock performances, followed by a late-night club at weekends.

JJ Smyth's, 12 Aungier St, **T** 01 475 2565. *Daily from 2100. €6. Map 2, D6, p248* Nightly blues and jazz sessions are held above an unreconstructed local pub.

Olympia Theatre, 72 Dame St, **T** 01 677 7744. *Box office Mon-Sat 1030-1830. €10-30. Map 3, D4, p250* This lovely old music hall hosts tribute bands, rock legends, stand-up comics and the occasional play. Seats are removed for big gigs and three bars keep the punters in party mood.

The Point, East Link Bridge, **T** 01 836 3633. *Box office 1000-1800. Ticket prices vary. Map 1, D7, p247* Born-again Evangelists, rock bands and *Riverdance* all perform in this vast old train depot.

Shelter@Vicar Street/Vicar Street, 99 Vicar St, **T** 01 454 6656. *Mon-Sat from 1930. Admission varies. Map 2, B2, p248* These adjoining venues are two of the most important destinations on Dublin's live music circuit. Vicar Street holds about 500 and hosts some big names; Shelter is smaller and is a good place to listen to traditional music and jazz in intimate surroundings.

Temple Bar Music Centre, Curved St, **T** 01 670 9202, www.tbmc.ie *Daily from 1930. Ticket prices vary. Map 3, C6, p250* The packed programme features everything from trad Irish music to salsa dancing and the occasional late-night concert.

Whelan's, 25 Wexford St, **T** 01 478 0766. *Mon-Sat from 2030. €10-20. Map 2, E6, p248* One of the city's best live music venues is located in a converted warehouse at the back of a 19th-century pub. It's big but comfortable.

Classical music and opera

While pop music rocks the night away in Dublin's clubland, classical music is a rather less obvious feature of the city's cultural landscape; you'll need to keep an eye on listings in the *Event Guide* or *In Dublin* to track down concerts and recitals.

The city has two resident orchestras, the **National Symphony Orchestra**, **T** 01 208 3347, and the **RTÉ Concert Orchestra**, **T** 01 208 3347, both of which perform at the National Concert Hall. Look out for the biannual seasons by **Opera Ireland**, **T** 01 208 3347, at the Gaiety Theatre (p171) and frequent recitals of Irish chamber music at the Dublin City Gallery by the **Concorde Ensemble**, **T** 091 522 867. Occasional concerts are held at Christchurch (p52) and St Patrick's (p56), the Irish Museum of Modern Art (p54), the Project Arts Centre (p172) and St Stephen's Church, Mount St Upper, **T** 01 288 0663.

▶ The Helix

Until recently, if you went to a show in Dublin you'd end up in an old bus depot, an Edwardian music hall, a brutalist concrete box or some other adapted space, peering round badly placed pillars, straining to hear the music, fighting for elbow room at the bar in the interval. In the cramped, land-hungry city that Dublin has become, the expenditure of space and hard cash on a performing arts centre is a rare and wonderful thing. Two years in the building and many more than that in the planning, the eagerly awaited **Helix** (Collins Avenue, Glasnevin, **T** 01 700 7000, www.thehelix.ie) opened on the campus of Dublin City University in October 2002.

This new, state-of-the-art complex, designed by the architects A&D Wejchert, consists of three performance venues: a small intimate space, called imaginatively, The Space, a larger more conventional theatre (guess what that's called) for operas, plays and dance, and the huge Mahony concert hall, reputed to seat twelve hundred or so audience members. The three venues are linked by a vast three-level lobby area, which makes beautiful use of light and space to draw the eye and the visitor deeper into the building.

Design aside, the new theatre is going to change the face of the performing arts scene in Dublin, attracting all kinds of people to a single venue: rock-music lovers, theatre buffs, opera groupies and families. It may never be as cutting-edge as the Project in Temple Bar or have the history of the Abbey, but already in its first few months it has offered *La Traviata*, *Carmen*, several visiting orchestras, chamber music, ballet, mainstream and alternative theatre, an RTÉ radio comedy improv show, an ice-dance performance, gigs by Van Morrison and Hugh Cornwell (late of the Stranglers) and the finals of the vastly popular RTÉ *You're a Star* show.

Bank of Ireland Arts Centre, Foster Pl, **T** 01 671 488. *Box office Tue-Fri 1100-1600. Map 2, A7, p249* Free lunchtime concerts are held during the winter months, supplemented by classical music evenings and poetry readings.

Dublin City Gallery 'Hugh Lane', Parnell Sq, **T** 01 874 1903. *Sun 1200. Map 5, E5, p252* Free concerts are held here in a spacious auditorium from September to June.

National Concert Hall, Earlsfort Terr, **T** 01 475 1572, www.nch.ie *Box office Mon-Sat 1000-1900. Map 2, F8, p249* The former Great Hall of University College Dublin (now located out of town at Belfield) is the city's main venue for classical orchestral performances. However, what the building gains in historical and architectural interest is sadly lost in the less-than-excellent acoustics. Tickets are usually available up to three months in advance and can be booked online.

Royal Dublin Showgrounds Concert Hall, Merrion Rd, Ballsbridge, **T** 01 668 0866. *Box office Mon-Fri 0900-1700. Map 4, E4, p251* Occasional orchestral, chamber music and opera performances take place in a big and rather bland environment.

Theatre

The **Dublin Theatre Festival** takes place in autumn (p177), when international and local productions are performed throughout the city and every hotel is bursting at the seams. It is preceded by the Fringe Festival when the wackier elements of modern theatre predominate. Even if you aren't visiting the city at festival time, you'll find plenty of drama on offer. The city's theatres are flourishing, from the traditional **Abbey Theatre** to the innovative **Project Arts Centre**, where art, dance, theatre and video meet.

Street theatre
Buskers pull in the crowds on Grafton Street.

Abbey Theatre, 26 Abbey St Lower, **T** 01 878 7222,
www.abbeytheatre.ie *Box office Mon-Sat 1000-1900. Map 5, G8,
p253* One of the most famous theatres in the world was rebuilt
in the 1960s in a brutalist style that will tremendously disappoint
theatrical pilgrims drawn here by tales of the Abbey's stirring role
in the city's history. Opened as a theatre in 1902 by the poet WB
Yeats and his friend Lady Gregory, the Abbey staged cutting-edge
drama that outraged public opinion by depicting Irish life in all its
diversity. Nowadays, however, the choice of material and the style
of productions tend to err on the safe side. The current ugly and
uncomfortable venue is due to be rebuilt in 2005.

! A performance of JM Synge's *The Playboy of the Western World*
at the Abbey Theatre in 1904 caused riots in the streets after
one of the actresses appeared in her shift on the stage.

Andrew's Lane Studio and Theatre , 9-13 Andrew's Lane,
T 01 679 5720. *Box office Mon-Sat 1030-1900. Map 2, B7, p249*
Somewhat faded venue for popular theatre. Regional touring
companies and the occasional international troupe perform
sound but unchallenging stuff.

Bewley's Café Theatre, Grafton St, **T** 086 878 4001.
€10 including lunch. Map 2, C7, p249 Lunchtime theatre
is sometimes performed upstairs in beautiful Bewley's. The
productions are often surprisingly innovative.

Crypt Arts Centre, Dublin Castle, Dame Lane, **T** 01 671 3387.
Box office Mon-Fri 1000-1800. €10. Map 3, E3, p250 This intimate
space in the crypt of Dublin Castle's church is used by smaller,
avant-garde theatre companies.

Dublin Writers' Museum, Parnell Sq, **T** 01 872 2077. *Box office
Mon-Sat 1000-1700. Map 5, E6, p252* Decent productions of classic
Irish theatre.

Gaiety Theatre, South King St, **T** 01 677 1717. *Box office
Mon-Sat 1000-1900. €17-30. Map 2, C7, p249* A bums-on-seats
kind of place, the Gaiety is a little shabby round the edges and
home to all manner of beasts from Opera Ireland (p167) to panto
to funny movies on club nights (p152).

Gate Theatre, 1 Cavendish Row, **T** 01 874 4045. *Box office
Mon-Sat 1000-1900. €20. Map 5, F6, p252* Dublin's second-most
famous theatre was founded in 1928 by Micheál MacLiammóir
and Hilton Edwards, an openly gay couple who defied sexual
conventions. MacLiammóir performed in over 300 roles at the
Gate between the 1920s and the 1970s, and the theatre staged
Oscar Wilde's *Salome* after the play had been banned in Britain.
It's a little more conservative these days and less inclined to host

'progressive plays unfettered by theatrical convention', but the Gate remains a fine theatre with a pleasantly balcony- and box-free auditorium.

Peacock Theatre, 26 Abbey St Lower, **T** 01 878 7222. *Box office Mon-Sat 1000-1900. Map 5, F6, p252* The experimental wing of the Abbey, the Peacock mixes established drama with previously unproduced works by young Irish writers.

Project, 39 East Essex St, Temple Bar, **T** 1850 260 027, www.project.ie *Box office Mon-Sat 1000-1700. €10-15. Map 3, D4, p250* Purpose-built in 2000, this performing arts centre is the best place to catch something new and experimental on the stage. Two theatres and an exhibition space host live music (including occasional jazz weekends), art, dance, video and film work as well as more conventional theatre.

Samuel Beckett Centre, Trinity College, **T** 01 608 2266. *Box office Mon-Fri 1100-1800. €4-20. Map 2, A8, p249* Work by students of Trinity and UCD, as well as other theatre groups.

The biggest event in the city's calendar is St Patrick's Day, which brings hordes of visitors to the city for a boozy, week-long party. Another highlight is Bloomsday, which celebrates the city's most famous writer and his most famous literary creation, and attracts Joyce enthusiasts as well as people who've never read *Ulysses*, but just enjoy dressing up. Other large-scale events include the film and theatre festivals in March and September, and the marathon in October.

Book your flight, accommodation and car hire well in advance, if you're visiting Dublin during a major event, as the city's hotels fill up quickly and rates often rise to coincide with key dates in the city's cultural and sporting calendar.

February

Rugby Six Nations Championship (weekends in February and March) The Irish home games of the annual rugby competition between Ireland, England, Scotland, Wales, France and Italy are held at Lansdowne Road Stadium (p195). Tickets cost between €20 and €50. Fans don't just come to Dublin for the live matches, however; they also come to watch televised games in the pubs of Temple Bar, regardless of which country the match is being played in.

March

Dublin Film Festival (early March) Movies in various genres are screened at all the major cinemas around town. Tickets should be booked in advance. For further information 'phone **T** 01 679 2937 or consult www.dublinff.com

St Patrick's Day Festival (the week leading up to the 17th March) Once a religious event marked by a few dreary processions, St Patrick's Day is now a full-on, week-long festival. In 2003, 300,000 Dubliners and visitors filled the streets of the city to enjoy green beer, a professional parade, street performers, a music festival, fireworks and copious amounts of Guinness. For further information 'phone **T** 01 676 3205 or consult www.paddyfest.ie

April

Handel's Messiah (exact date varies) The very first performance of the *Messiah* took place on Fishamble Street in Dublin in 1792. This historic event is commemorated each year with a performance in Neal's Music Hall. For further information 'phone **T** 01 677 2255.

Convergence Festival (last week in April) A celebration of green issues in Temple Bar, centred around international Earth Day. For further information 'phone **T** 01 677 2255.

May

Diversions (May-August) A wide variety of events takes place in Meeting House Square, Temple Bar, throughout the summer, ranging from music and dance performances to film screenings and kids stuff on Sunday afternoons. For further information 'phone **T** 01 677 2255 or consult www.templebar.ie

June

Evening Herald Women's Mini-Marathon (date varies) A 16-km charity event that attracts lots of silly entries and general good fun. For further information 'phone **T** 01 496 0861.

Bloomsday (12th-16th June) Bloomsday celebrates the day (16th June 1904) on which Joyce's novel *Ulysses* is set. Now expanded into a five-day festival, it incorporates Joyce-related readings, performances, dressing-up and dramatized walks around the city following the route of the novel's main character, Leopold Bloom. For further information 'phone **T** 01 878 8547.

Gay Pride (late June weekend) A parade and other events to celebrate the city's gay and lesbian population. For further information consult www.gcn.ie

July

Dublin Jazz Festival (first week in July) Plenty of live jazz performances take place in Temple Bar and other locations. For further information 'phone **T** 01 670 3885.

Anna Livia Opera Festival (mid July) Opera performances are held at the Olympia Theatre, Bank of Ireland Arts Centre and other locations. For further information 'phone **T** 01 661 7544 or consult www.operaannalivia.com

Gay and Lesbian Film Festival (late July/early August) This four-day annual festival has been running for more than a decade and features movie screenings, parties, lectures and an awards ceremony. For further information 'phone **T** 01 473 0599 or consult www.gcn.ie/dlgff

August

Kerrygold Horse Show (early August) A five-day showjumping event at the Royal Dublin Showground. The highlight is the Kerrygold Nations Cup in which teams compete for the Aga Khan Trophy. For further information 'phone **T** 01 668 0866.

Liffey Swim (late August/early September) Four hundred or so contestants swim the 1½ miles from Rory O'More Bridge to the Custom House Quay, trying to avoid all manner of hazards, not least the state of the water they are swimming in. Spectators line the bridges and the Boardwalk to watch.

September

Dublin Theatre Festival (late September-early October) This is one of the city's biggest annual events, with a fringe festival running at the same time. High-quality international productions are supplemented by lots of experimental theatre performances. For further information 'phone **T** 01 877 8434 or consult www.dublintheatrefestival.com

Horsing around
Celebrating a Christmas win at Leopardstown Racecourse.

October

Dublin Marathon (late Oct) 26 miles (42 km) and thousands of runners. For further information 'phone **T** 01 670 7918 or consult www.dublincitymarathon.ie

Samhain (31st Oct) Dublin's Hallowe'en festival features a parade, street theatre, fireworks, dance and music. For further information 'phone **T** 01 855 7154 or consult www.visitdublin.com

December

Christmas Racing Festival (26th-29th Dec) Four days of steeplechasing events at Leopardstown Racecourse (p195).

People tend not to be drawn to Dublin for the shopping, although once in the city they'll find plenty of opportunities to part with some serious cash. Visitors from across the Irish Sea might be convinced they're still in Manchester or Basildon, thanks to the number of British high-street shops clustered around Grafton Street, but Dublin is also home to some splendid old-fashioned, home-grown department stores such as Roches or Arnotts that are fun to explore. Prices might raise a few eyebrows, though. No bargains for Brits here.

Where Dublin excels in the shopping stakes is in locally crafted goodies from woolly jumpers to hand-woven rugs, and from gorgeous pots to elegant furniture, glass, jewellery and fashions. Beautiful, covetable items from all over Ireland are sold in Dublin through dedicated sales shops and in the big craft stores on Nassau Street.

Dublin will also delight lovers of vintage clothing and anyone who enjoys poking around antiques shops looking for bargains. And no one should miss the unique atmosphere of Dublin's street markets.

The two main shopping areas are based around **Grafton Street** and **Henry Street**. Each has a distinctly different tone: Grafton Street is definitely the more upmarket of the two, with a number of quality boutiques among the high-street chains; Henry Street is a little seedy in places, but has an excellent street market and good shops in the adjoining arcades.

Antiques

One of the best parts of town for antique shopping is Francis Street, where you'll find a whole cluster of shops selling antiques and bric-a-brac.

Coyle Antiques, 74 Francis St, **T** 01 454 2696. *Mon-Sat 1100-1700. Map 2, C3, p248* Domestic 19th- and 20th-century furniture, pottery and paintings.

Esther Sexton Antiques, 51 Francis St, **T** 01 473 0909 *Mon-Sat 1100-1700. Map 2, C3, p248* Edwardian and Victorian furniture.

Gordon Nichol, 67-8 Francis St, **T** 01 454 3322 *Mon-Sat 1130-1730. Map 2, B3, p248* Furniture and architectural fittings.

Powerscourt Centre, 59 South William St, **T** 01 679 4144. *Mon-Wed, Fri and Sat 1000-1800, Thu 1000-2000, Sun 1200-1800. Map 2, B7, p249* The first floor of this upmarket shopping arcade has half-a-dozen classy antique shops selling antique jewellery, decorations and furniture. There are no big bargains here, but lots of authenticity.

Renaissance, 41 Camden St, **T** 01 475 2461. *Mon-Wed, Fri, Sat 1100-1800, Thu 1100-2100, Sun 1400-1800. Map 2, F6, p248* More at the junk end of the market, with chandeliers, mirrors, furniture, paintings, old pub fittings and bric-a-brac.

Art

Artselect, Meeting House Sq, Temple Bar, **T** 01 635 1046, www.artselect.ie *Mon-Sat 1000-1730. Map 3, D5, p250* Various forms of artwork are on sale here, from watercolours and oil on canvas to photographs, multi-media pieces, sculpture, kinetic art, ceramics and glasswork.

The Bridge, 6 Ormond Quay Upper, **T** 01 872 9702, www.thebridgegallery.com *Mon-Sat 1000-1800, Sun 1400-1700. Map 3, B2, p250* This is primarily a commercial gallery with 2,000 sq ft of exhibition space on two floors, but it's fronted by an art and craft shop selling gifts and framed watercolours and oils.

Giles Norman, Powerscourt Centre, 59 South William St, **T** 01 677 3455, www.gilesnorman *Mon-Wed, Fri and Sat 1000-1800, Thu 1000-2000, Sun1200-1800 Map 3, B7, p250* Black and white photos of Dublin and Ireland by Giles Norman.

James Gallery, 4 Exchequer St, **T** 01 677 4599. *Mon-Sat 1000-1830, Sun 1100-1800. Map 2, B6, p248* Contemporary Irish art.

Merrion Square *Map 2, C10/11, p249* At weekends this is a great place to look for original art works at bargain prices. As well as the tearful pierrots, cute street urchins with seriously over-large eyes and painted velvet pieces, the outdoor displays include some interesting amateur art, with the painters often on hand to tell you all about it.

Original Print Gallery, 4 Temple Bar, **T** 01 677 3183, www.originalprint.ie *Tue-Fri 1030-1730, Sat 1100-1700, Sun 1400-1800. Map 3, C5, p250* A collection of prints by Irish and international artists.

Temple Bar Gallery and Studios, 5-9 Temple Bar, **T** 01 671 0073, www.templebargallery.com *Mon, Wed, Fri and Sat 1000-1800, Thu 1400-1900, Sun 1400-1800. Map 3, C5, p250* This spot hosts commercial art exhibitions with very high price tags, although the Multiples Gallery on the same site sells prints and lesser-known artists' works at carry-out prices. The working studios can be visited on request.

Books and maps

Books Upstairs, 36 College Green, **T** 01 679 6687, www.books irish.com *Mon-Fri 1000-1900, Sat 1000-1800, Sun 1300-1800. Map 2, A7, p249* The sort of place where you're always ducking out of other people's way, but with a good selection of material.

Cathach Books, 10 Duke St, **T** 01 671 8676. *Mon-Sat 0930-1745. Map 2, B8, p249* Antiquarian bookseller dealing in Irish-interest titles and native writers. It has signed first editions by all sorts of people as well as old maps and prints.

Eason's, 40 O'Connell St, **T** 01 858 3800, www.eason.ie *Mon-Wed and Sat 0830-1845, Thu 0830-2045, Fri 0830-1945, Sun 1245-1745. Map 5, G7, p253* Wide-ranging magazine section, a good choice of maps and guide books, plus stationery, art supplies, videos and DVDs.

Hodges Figgis, 56-8 Dawson St, **T** 01 677 4754. *Mon-Wed and Fri 0900-1900, Thur 0900-2000, Sat 0900-1800, Sun 1200-1800. Map 2, B8, p249* The maze-like interior has poky little spaces for browsing in, an enormous range of material and a smart café.

Hughes & Hughes, Stephen's Green Shopping Centre, **T** 01 478 3060. *Mon-Wed, Fri and Sat 0930-1800, Thu 0930-2000, Sun 1200-1800. Map 2, C7, p249* Reasonable range of books, with especially good children's and Irish interest sections.

National Map Centre, 34 Aungier St, **T** 01 476 0471, www.mapcentre.ie *Mon-Fri 0900-1700. Map 2, D6, p248* Surprise, surprise, this is the place to buy a map.

Waterstone's, 7 Dawson St, **T** 01 679 1415. *Mon-Wed and Fri 0900-2000, Thu 0900-2030, Sat 0900-1900, Sun 0900-1800. Map 2, B8, p249* A well laid-out branch that stocks all the pulp fiction you've ever wanted. It's strong on books with an Irish angle.

Winding Stair, 40 Ormond Quay, **T** 01 873 3292, www.windingstair.ie *Mon-Sat 1000-1800, Sun 1300-1800. Map 3, A6, p250* Good second-hand books are stocked over three floors, and there's a laid-back café overlooking the river.

Crafts

Individually crafted ceramics, glass, wood, textiles and furniture are sold upstairs at the Designyard (p187).

Blarney Woollen Mills, 21-3 Nassau St, **T** 01 671 0066, www.blarneywoollenmills.ie *Mon-Wed, Fri and Sat 0900-1800, Thu 0900-2000, Sun 1100-1800. Map 2, B8, p249* The usual barrage of hand-woven clothes, hand-knitted accessories and leprechaun designs. Some good bargains to be had if you poke around.

Cleo Ltd, 18 Kildare St, **T** 01 676 1421. *Mon-Wed, Fri and Sat 0930-1800, Thu 0930-2000. Map 2, C9, p249* Slightly upmarket versions of the products sold at Blarney Woollen Mills.

Dublin Woollen Mills, 41 Ormond Quay Lower, **T** 01 677 5014, www.woollenmills.com *Mon-Wed, Fri and Sat 0930-1800, Thu 0900-2000, Sun 1300-1800. Map 3, A6, p250* Cheaper clone of Blarney Woollen Mills, retailing jumpers, pots, tablecloths, embellished tea towels, scented candles and stuff of that ilk.

House of Ireland, 38 Nassau St, **T** 01 671 6133,
www.houseofireland.com *Mon-Wed, Fri and Sat 0900-1800, Thu
0900-2000, Sun 1030-1800. Map 2, B8, p249* Irish fine china, crystal,
woollens, hand-made cloth and leather goods.

Kilkenny Shop, 6 Nassau St, **T** 01 677 7066, www.kilkenny
group.com *Mon-Wed, Fri and Sat 0900-1800, Thu 0900-2000,
Sun 1000-1800. Map 2, B8, p249* This is one of the better stores
for buying Irish-made items, including very classy woollens,
hand-woven clothes and crafts. It also has a great café upstairs.

Whichcraft, Lord Edward St, Cow's Lane, Temple Bar, **T** 01 670
9371, 01 474 1011, www.whichcraft.com *Mon-Sat 0900-1800,
Sun 1000-1800. Map 3, E3, p250* Covetable hand-made furniture,
jewellery and decorations. Many pieces are one-offs.

Department stores

Arnotts , 12 Henry St, **T** 01 872 1111, www.arnotts.ie *Mon-Wed,
Fri and Sat 0900-1830, Thu 0900-2130, Sun 1200-1800. Map 5, G6,
p252* This huge old department store has been modernized a
little round the edges with a coffee bar and trendier clothes,
but remains just as chaotic as ever at its heart.

Brown Thomas, 88-95 Grafton St. **T** 01 605 6666. *Mon-Wed,
Fri and Sat 0900-1800, Thu 0900-2000, Sun1200-1800. Map 2, C7,
p249* The poshest department store in Dublin is worth a look for
its designer fashions. It gets a mention in James Joyce's *Ulysses*.

Clery's, 18-27 O'Connell St, **T** 01 878 6000, www.clerys.com
Mon-Wed, Fri and Sat 0900-1800, Thu 0900-2100 Map 5, G8, p253
Clery's dominates O'Connell Street with its vast Selfridges-style
window displays and enormous range of goods. Reasonable prices,
lots of Irish gifts and a café upstairs.

Debenham's, Jervis Centre, Jervis St, **T** 01 878 1222. *Map 5, G6, p252* This British department store nestles in a recently built shopping centre and has particularly good designer concessions.

Dunnes, Henry St, **T** 01 671 4629, www.dunnesstores.ie
Mon-Wed, Fri, Sat 0900-1800, Thu 0900-2100, Sun 1400-1800.
Map 5, G6, p252 The Irish equivalent of Marks and Spencer stocks sensible clothes and homewares. There are additional branches in Grafton Street and around the city.

Roches, 54 Henry St, **T** 01 873 0044 *Mon-Wed, Fri and Sat 0900-1800, Thu 0900-2100.* *Map 5, B6, p252* Roches is best for household stuff, such as bedlinen and kitchen accessories, but has good clothing sections, too.

Fashion

Grafton Street has all the international women's clothing chains that you'd expect, plus a couple of Irish ones, such as **A Wear** and **O'Connor's**. Temple Bar offers outdoor gear, vintage clothing and wackier street fashions, while Henry Street has another rash of chain stores. Among the department stores, **Brown Thomas** has upmarket designer concessions, while **Debenham's** has a good choice of labels at respectable prices. Lovers of recycled fashions should head for the string of charity shops along South Great George's, Aungier and Wexford Streets.

A Wear, 26 Grafton St, **T** 01671 7200. *Mon-Wed, Fri, Sat 0900-1800, Thu 0900-2030, Sun 1200-1800.* *Map 2, C7, p249*
Clothes for young Dubliners, including lots of Irish designs.

BT2, 28-9 Grafton St, **T** 01 605 6707. *Mon-Wed 1000-1830, Thu 1000-2000, Fri and Sat 1000-1900, Sun 1200-1800.* *Map 2, C7, p249*
Young and trendy offshoot of Brown Thomas, with designer labels.

Costume, 10-11 Castle Market, **T** 01 679 5200. *Mon-Wed, Fri and Sat 1000-1800, Thu 1000-1900. Map 2, B6, p248* Elegant designs by local and European names.

Cuba, 13 Trinity St, **T** 01 672 7489. *Mon-Wed, Fri and Sat 0930-1800, Thu 0930-2000, Sun 1200-1800. Map 5, F5, p252* Designer gear for the young and streetwise.

Louise Kennedy, 56 South Merrion Sq, **T** 01 662 0056. *Mon-Fri 0900-1800, Sat 0930-1800. Map 2, D10, p249* Designs by the big name in Irish fashion, plus glassware, leather things and wooden furniture by David Linley.

O'Connor's, ILAC Centre, **T** 01 872 9902. *Mon-Wed, Fri, Sat 0930-1800, Thu 0930-2100. Map 5, G6, p252* Plenty of fashionable denim. There's another branch in Grafton Street.

Smock, East Essex St, **T** 01 613 9000. *Mon-Wed, Fri and Sat 1030-1800, Thu 1030-1900. Map 3, C4, p250* Tiny boutique with lots of Irish-designed material at reasonable prices.

Urban Outfitters, Cecilia House, Temple Bar, **T** 01 670 6202. *Mon-Wed and Sat 1000-1900, Thu and Fri 1000-2000, Sun 1200-1800. Map 3, C6, p250* Ultra-cool clothing and accessories, plus nifty homewares and dance music.

Wild Child, 61 South Great George's St, **T** 01 475 5099. *Mon-Wed, Fri and Sat 1000-1800, Thu 1000-1900. Map 2, B6, p248* Stylish second-hand clothes with prices to match.

Jewellery

Designyard, 12 East Essex St, Temple Bar, **T** 01 677 8453, www.designyard.ie *Mon, Wed-Sat 1000-1730, Tue 1100-1730.*

Map 3, C4, p250 Unique pieces of jewellery are individually designed and exhibited here.

Powerscourt Centre, 59 South William St, **T** 01 679 4144. *Mon-Wed, Fri and Sat 1000-1800, Thu 1000-2000, Sun 1200-1800.* *Map 2, B7, p249* On the first floor look out for Michael Perry, Emma-Stewart Liberty, Patrick Flood, Ladybird Jewel, while on the ground floor are Appleby and Equinox.

Rhinestones, 18 Andrew St, **T** 01 679 0759. *Mon-Wed, Fri and Sat 0930-1800, Thu 0930-2000.* *Map 2, B7, p249* Wonderful collection of stylish antique jewellery, which is often much more desirable than the modern stuff.

Food and drink

Big Cheese Company, 12 and 15 Trinity St, **T** 01 671 1399. *Mon-Fri 1000-1830, Sat 0930-1800.* *Map 5, F5, p252* Cheesy choices including speciality rural Irish varieties.

Blazing Salads, 42 Drury St, **T** 01 671 9552. *Mon-Fri 0900-1800, Sat 0900-1730.* *Map 2, B6, p248* Lovely vegetarian delicatessen and bakery close to Grafton Street. Serves an extensive daily menu of takeout lunch items – veggieburgers, spring rolls, pizza, salads and soups – as well as organic bread and deli goodies.

Gallic Kitchen, 49 Francis St, **T** 01 454 4912. *Mon-Sat 0900-1700.* *Map 2, C3, p248* Ready-to-eat potato cakes, quiches, pies and cakes, plus cheese and other tasty treats. Look out for the stall in the Temple Bar market on Saturdays.

Magill's Delicatessen, 14 Clarendon St, **T** 01 671 3830. *Mon- Sat 0900-1700.* *Map 2, C7, p249* Asian and continental delicacies.

Sheridan's Cheesemonger, 11 South Ann St, **T** 01 679 3143. *Mon-Sat 0900-1700. Map 2, C7, p253* Lots of Irish and continental cheeses. Try before you buy.

Markets

Blackrock, Main St, Blackrock, **T** 01 283 3522. *Sat 1100-1730, Sun 1200-1730.* Enclosed in a courtyard, this trendy market sells alternative fashions, pots, paintings, mirrors, antiques, scented candles, Navajo dreamcatchers and more. A perfect place, then, to find something to take home for the relatives.

Camden Street. *Daily. Map 2, F6, p248* A genuine working street market selling fruit and veg, flowers and sports gear. The road here isn't pedestrianized so the stalls are crammed onto the pavement.

George's Street Arcade. *Daily. Map 2, B6, p248* A covered market full of alternative clothes, second-hand books, exotic foodstuffs, CDs and records, some inexpensive jewellery and a cheap café.

Meeting House Square, Temple Bar. *Sat. Map 3, D5, p250* Knobbly-looking vegetables, goat's cheese, fresh vine leaves, olives and so on are sold by stallholders with dishevelled hair and woolly jumpers.

Moore Street. *Daily. Map 5, G6, p252* Dublin's most famous market spreads out into Henry Street with stalls selling fruit and vegetables, cigarette lighters, cheap jewellery, sports gear and lots more. A great place to experience life's rich tapestry and north Dublin accents.

Shopping

Miscellaneous

Hemp Store, 167 Capel St, **T** 01 874 8515, www.dublinhemp.com
Mon-Fri 1100-1800, Thu 1100-1900. *Map 5, G5, p252* Nearly
everything at this shop is made from hemp: bedlinen, jackets,
candles, wallets, strange teas and cosmetics. It's the kind of place
that can now be seen in most large cities around the world.

Music

There are big branches of **Virgin Records** and **HMV** in both
Henry Street and Grafton Street. Both have huge stocks and regular
sales, but they are not the cheapest places in town.

Celtic Note, 14-15 Nassau St, **T** 01 670 4157, www.celticnote.ie
Mon-Sat 0930-1830, Sun 1100-1800. *Map 2, B8, p249* Stocks Irish
music of all descriptions and is well worth checking out.

Golden Discs, 8 North Earl St, **T** 01 874 0417. *Mon-Wed and Fri
0930-1830, Thu 0930-2000, Sat 0900-1800, Sun 1400-1800.* *Map 5,
G7, p253* Huge range of music and videos at better-than-big-name
prices. There are also branches at St Stephen's Green West, Grafton
Street and 31 Mary Street.

Smile Records, 59 South Great George's St, **T** 01 478 2005.
Mon-Sat 1100-1900, Sun 1300-1800. *Map 2, B6, p248* Second-hand
music and books.

Walton's, 70 South Great George's St, **T** 01 475 0661, and 2 North
Frederick St, **T** 01 874 7805. *Mon-Sat 0900-1800, Sun 1200-1700.*
Map 2, B6, p248 New and second-hand musical instruments
(especially Irish instruments) as well as CDs, cassettes and books.

Ireland's national sports are hurling and Gaelic football, ancient games that are hugely exciting to watch. Soccer, rugby and horse racing are also very popular, with tickets for big events selling out fast.

For the active visitor, Dublin offers a whole host of sports from high-adrenaline activities like abseiling, go-karting and paragliding to more sedate pastimes. Dublin's location on the coast ensures a full range of water-based activities, while inland there are numerous golf courses that are increasingly taking over the countryside around the city. The public parks have pitches marked out for hurling, football and rugby, as well as basketball and tennis courts, which are all free to the public.

Adventure sports

Adventure Activities Ltd, 5 Trintonville Ave, **T** 01 668 8047.
Map 4, A7, p251 High-adrenaline sports in and around Dublin.
Phone for rates.

Hang-gliding and Paragliding Centre, Kilmacanogue, Co
Wicklow, **T** 01 830 3884. Take to the skies south of the city.
Phone for rates.

Sea Safari, Malahide Marina, Malahide, **T** 01 806 1626,
www.seasafari.ie *Daily depending on the weather. €25 per person,
€80 family. Minimum age 8.* Cruise the coast in a rigid inflatable
with full wet gear provided. The one-hour 'thrill seeker' is fast and
furious, but there are more leisurely options.

Gaelic football and hurling

Croke Park, Jones Rd, Drumcondra, **T** 01 836 3222, www.gaa.ie
Ticket office Mon-Fri 0900-1730. Ticket prices vary. *Map 5, B9, p253*
This the home of the Gaelic Athletic Association, which governs
both Gaelic football and hurling, and hosts major club and county
matches. Tickets, which may be upwards of €12 for a high-profile
competition, go on sale via the website up to ten days before a
match. No phone bookings. See also p194.

Go-karting

Kylemore Indoor Karting, Killeen Rd, Killeen, **T** 01 626 1444,
www.kylemore-karting.com *Daily 1000-late. €15-30.* Karts travel
at up to 40 mph around two tracks, allowing boy and girl racers to
speed around 20 times in ten minutes. Helmets, gloves, racing
suits and training are provided.

Gaelic games

Despite the fuss over Roy Keane and Irish soccer's World Cup effort in 2002, Gaelic football and hurling remain Ireland's undisputed national sports. Both games involve teams of 15 players, a pitch similar to a soccer pitch and goals that are a cross between soccer and rugby posts.

Gaelic football has been played in one form or another for a few hundred years, although its current rules were not laid down until 1885 by the Gaelic Athletic Association, a sporting scion of the late 19th-century Gaelic cultural revival. The game is similar to Aussie Rules football with players using both their hands and their feet to pass the ball.

Hurling has an even longer pedigree, dating back 2,000 years. The pre-Christian 'Brehon Laws' awarded compensation to the families of those injured during hurling matches, and the battle of Moytura, fought in 200 BC, is said to have begun as a hurling match. To the untutored eye hurling looks a lot like hockey or shinty, but it is much faster. The players hold vicious-looking wooden sticks, which are wider at one end and are used to either carry or pass the ball.

Every small town in Ireland has both hurling and Gaelic football teams and local rivalries can be fierce. Gaelic footballers often play for the town soccer team, too.

Golf

Edmonstown Golf Club, Rathfarnham, **T** 01 493 1082, www.edmonstowngolfclub.ie €55 Mon-Fri, €65 Sat and Sun. This 18-hole golf course is close to Dublin city centre, and is surrounded by pretty parkland with the Wicklow Mountains as a striking backdrop.

Greyhound racing

Both courses in Dublin have been recently upgraded to offer a full evening's entertainment, with restaurants and bars to supplement the racing and betting.

Harold's Cross Racetrack, 151 Harold's Cross Rd, **T** 01 497 1081. *Mon, Tue and Fri from 2000. €7.*

Shelbourne Park Stadium, Lotts Rd, Ringsend, **T** 01 668 3502. *Wed, Thu and Sat from 2000. €7.* *Map 1, E7, p247*

Horse racing

Leopardstown Racecourse, Foxrock, **T** 01 289 3607, www.leopardstown.com *Grandstand €12-16.* Twenty-two fixtures – a mixture of national hunt and flat racing – are held here each year. The best events are the four-day Leopardstown Festival, which starts on St Stephen's Day (Boxing Day; p178), and the weekend meetings throughout June and July.

Ice-skating

In December and January there are open-air ice rinks at Smithfield and beside the river at North Wall Quay.

Rugby

Lansdowne Road Stadium, Lansdowne Rd, Ballsbridge, **T** 01 668 9300. *Ticket office Mon-Fri 0900-1700. €4-60.* *Map 4, B4, p251* International matches take place here from August to May. Details are available from the Irish Rugby Football Union, **T** 01 668 4601, www.irfu.ie

Sailing

Irish National Sailing School, Marine Activity Centre, West Pier, Dun Laoghaire, **T** 01 284 4195, www.inss.ie Intensive sailing courses around Dun Laoghaire harbour are offered throughout the year. Phone for prices.

Swimming

National Aquatic Centre, Snugborough Road, Blanchardstown, **T** 01 646 4300, www.nac.ie *Leisure pool Mon-Fri 1100-2200, Sat and Sun 0900-2000. €9/€10 adults, €7/€8 concessions, €25.60/€30.60 family.* State-of-the-art water complex with lots of rides, including a water roller coaster, surfing machine, wave pool, bubble pool, a pirate ship, water slide and flume. Facilities also include a competition-standard pool and a diving pool.

Ten-pin bowling

Leisureplex, Malahide Rd, Coolock, **T** 01 848 5722. *Daily 24 hrs. €3.95 per game.* This place and its clones in Tallaght, **T** 01 459 9411, Blanchardstown, **T** 01 822 3030, and Stillorgan, **T** 01 288 1615, offer ten-pin bowling, quasar and pool. The Blanchardstown complex also has dodgems.

Windsurfing

Surfdock, Grand Canal Dockyard, South Docks Rd, Ringsend, **T** 01 668 3945 *Map 1, D7, p247* Lessons and equipment for hire. Facilities include a wind simulator. Phone for rates.

Fingall Windsurfing, Malahide, **T** 01 845 1979. Tuition and equipment hire. Phone for rates.

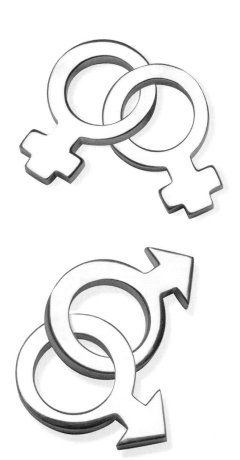

Technically, male homosexuality has only been legal in Ireland since 1993 when EC human rights legislation finally forced the Irish government to bring its policies up to date. In the same year the Irish government lowered the age of sexual consent to 17, making Ireland, for a time, more liberal than Britain. Gay women have never been outlawed in the same way as their practising male peers, since Queen Victoria decided that there could be no such thing as lesbianism.

There were, of course, gay- and gay-friendly venues in Dublin prior to 1993, which, in the age-old tradition of Irish solutions to Irish problems, were generally tolerated by the law enforcers as long as they kept a low profile. Since then, however, a whole pink economy has burgeoned in the city, largely generated by and aimed at gay men.

Resources

Garda Liaison Officer, Harcourt Street Garda Station, Harcourt St, **T** 01 666 3804, agecard@iol.ie. *Map 2, F6, p248*

Gay Men's Health Project, 19 Haddington Rd, **T** 01 660 2189, www.gayhealthnetwork.ie *Tue 1800-2030, Wed 1800-1930. Map 4, B1, p251* Free and confidential drop-in clinic.

Gay Switchboard, **T** 01 872 1055. *Sun-Fri 2000-2200.* Telephone advice and information.

Lesbian Line, **T** 01 872 9911. *Thu 1900-2100.* Telephone advice and information.

Outhouse, 105 Capel St, **T** 01 873 4932, www.outhouse.ie *Centre Mon-Fri 1000-1800. Coffee bar Mon-Fri 1300-1700. Map 5, G4, p252* A meeting place and resource centre for the lesbian and gay community. Check GCN for details of regular group meetings.

Swimmin Wimmin, **T** 01 834 8120. *Sun 1900.* A swimming group for gay women.

Media

Gay Community News (GCN) is a free, monthly, tabloid-sized newspaper dedicated to gay issues with listings for events all over Ireland. It is available from gay-friendly bars in Dublin, as well as from bookstores and, sometimes, the tourist office. Glossy magazine, **In Dublin** (p214) has a decent gay-interest section listing Dublin events, as does the fortnightly **Event Guide** (p214). It's also worth consulting the information and resources provided online at www.pinkpages.org and www.outhouse.ie

Accommodation

D Inn on the Liffey, 21 Ormond Quay, **T** 01 677 0828. *Map 3, B1, p250* Next door to Out on the Liffey pub (p201), this small hotel has en suite rooms with views of the river. Gay men only.

D Frankie's Guesthouse, 8 Camden Place, **T** 01 478 3087. www.frankiesguesthouse.com *Map 2, F6, p248* Comfortable mixed guest house in a salubrious area near St Stephen's Green.

Bars, clubs and club nights

In addition to a clutch of dedicated gay venues, Dublin has numerous bars and clubs that are 'gay friendly' or offer gay nights once or twice a week. However, venues and times frequently change, so it's a good idea to double check what's on before you sashay out in your boa and fishnets.

Candy, Pegs, Earl of Kildare Hotel, Kildare St, **T** 01 679 4388. *Thu and Sun 2300-0230. €8. Map 2, C9, p249* Loud and bright, Candy attracts a predominantly male clientele.

Front Lounge, 33-4 Parliament St, Temple Bar, **T** 01 670 4112. *Mon, Wed and Sun 1200-2330, Tue 1200-2400, Thu-Sat 1200-0130. Map 3, D3, p250* This gay-friendly spot features a karaoke night on Tuesday at 2200, hosted by Miss Panti.

The George, 89 South Great George's St, **T** 01 478 2983. *Wed-Sun 2200-0300. George free. Loft €8 after 2230. Map 2, B6, p248* This pub holds nightly gay-oriented events ranging from video screenings of *Queer as Folk* to pub quizzes. A highlight is bingo on Sundays, hosted by the now-famous TV drag queen, Shirley Temple Bar. Adjoining is the **Loft**, an intimate dance club.

GUBU, 7-8 Capel St, **T** 01 874 0710. *Mon-Wed 1700-2330, Thu-Sat 1700-0030, Sun 1600-2330. Map 5, H5, p252* Almost as popular as The George, GUBU makes a point of declaring itself 'straight friendly'. Its very modern, stark interior hosts stand-up comedy on Mondays after 2130 and live jazz on Sundays from 1700, followed by tarot readings after 2000.

HAM/Gristle, POD, Harcourt St, **T** 01 478 0225. *Fri 2300-late. €10. Map 2, F7, p249* Gristle is a gay karaoke night that takes place from 2100 every other Friday. Ham is a weekly club night for gay men only.

Hilton Edwards, Spy Club, Powerscourt Centre, South William St, **T** 01 677 0014. *Sun 2200-0300. €8. Map 2, B7, p249* This deeply glamorous gay lounge night is named after one half of Dublin's most famous queer couple and founder of the Gate Theatre (p171).

Libida, Chief O'Neill's, Smithfield, **T** 01 817 3838. *Last Sat of month. Free. Map 5, H2, p252* Lesbian night. Dates tend to vary, so check magazine listings or flyers at Outhouse.

Out on the Liffey, 27 Ormond Quay, **T** 01 872 2480. *Map 3, B1, p250* Quiet spot for a pink drink.

Slam@Switch, Eustace St, Temple Bar, **T** 01 670 7655. *Mon 2300- late. €8. Map 3, D5, p250* Two DJs on two floors entertain a gay and lesbian crowd at this popular Temple Bar club.

SPI Bar, 3 Eden Quay, **T** 01 874 6934. *Mon from 2300. Free. Map 5, H8, p253* A 'straight friendly' night. Other nights are labelled as 'gay friendly'.

Tracks, Oslo Bar, Connolly Station, **T** 01 703 1661. *2nd Sat of month. 2130 till late. Map 5, F11, p253* Monthly lesbian night.

Gay and lesbian

Pink calendar

March The St Patrick's Day festivities usually include a drag beauty pageant at the weekend, known as the Alternative Miss Ireland.

June Gay Pride Week is at the end of month, with gay ceilidhs, drag queen contests, theme nights and gay-interest theatre taking place in venues around town. Celebrations culminate with the Gay Pride Parade from O'Connell Street to Wood Quay.

July/August Week-long Lesbian and Gay Film Festival, hosted by the Irish Film Centre in Temple Bar (p161).

Wig & Pen, 131 Thomas St, **T** 01 677 3319. *Mon-Wed 1100-2330, Thu-Sat 1100-0030, Sun 1100-2300. Map 6, H12, p255* This newly reopened gay bar features women DJs on the decks on Fridays.

Saunas

The Boilerhouse, 12 Crane Lane, **T** 01 677 3130, www.the-boilerhouse.com *Mon-Wed 1300-1700, Thu 1300-0600, Fri 1300-Mon 0530. €13. Map 3, D4, p250* Sauna, steam rooms, solarium, private rooms, jacuzzi and café. For gay men only.

The Dock, 21 Ormond Quay Upper, **T** 01 872 4172. *Mon, Tue 1300-0130, Wed 1300-0300, Thu 1300-0500, Fri 1300-Mon 0500. Map 3, B1, p250* Located in the basement of the Inn on the Liffey, The Dock is a small sauna complex, without the facilities of The Boilerhouse. It's free to guests at the Inn. For gay men only.

Dublin is a child-friendly city, with large numbers of under-18s permanently resident here and plenty of amenities to cater for them, including interactive museums, sporting facilities and fun events. The city's proximity to beaches and countryside, not to mention the number of large green spaces in the centre, means there's ample opportunity for fair-weather activities.

Out of town are numerous destinations to grab a child's attention: Bray has amusement arcades, a seafront train and the National Seaworld Centre, as well as a beach, while Malahide Castle has enough attractions to entertain the whole family.

Kids

Sightseeing

The **Dublin Bus City Tour** (p28) will cart little legs painlessly around 16 of the city's major sights.

Chimney Viewing Tower, Smithfield Village, **T** 01 817 3800, www.chiefoneills.com *Mon-Sat 1000-1730, Sun 1100-1730. €5. Map 5, H2, p252* A lift takes you up to a viewing point at the top of the chimney. In December Santa makes this his home.

Dublinia, St Michael's Hill, Christchurch, **T** 01 679 4611, www.dublinia.ie *Apr-Sep, daily 1000-1700, Oct-Mar, Mon-Sat 1100-1630. €5.75. Map 2, B4, p248* Touchy feely history with a sense of fun. St Michael's Tower offers a great view of the city, but the long, steep staircase may be tiring for younger visitors.

Dublin Zoo, Phoenix Park, **T** 01 474 8900, www.dublinzoo.ie *Mar-Sep, Mon-Sat 0930-1800, Sun 1030-1800, Oct-Feb, Mon-Sat 0930-dusk, Sun 1030-dusk. Last admission 1 hr before closing. €10. Map 6, B6, p254* The recently refurbished zoo has a train ride and a hands-on city farm.

Fry Model Railway and Tara's Palace, Malahide Castle Demesne, Malahide, **T** 01 846 3779, www.visitdublin.com *Apr-Sep, Mon-Sat 1000-1300 and 1400-1700, Sun and public holidays 1400-1800. €2.* Children will love the model railway and doll's houses here. The tour of adjoining Malahide Castle (p99) includes a ghost story in the dining room, and there's a fab adventure playground on the estate.

National Museum of Decorative Arts and History, Collins Barracks, Benburb St, **T** 01 677 7444, www.museum.ie *Tue-Sat 1000-1700, Sun 1400-1700. Free. Guided tours €1.50.*

Kids

Map 6, F11, p255 Pull-open drawers, audio-visual displays and plenty more to keep little eyes and fingers busy.

National Museum of Natural History, Merrion St Upper, **T** 01 677 7444, www.museum.ie *Tue-Sat 1000-1700, Sun 1400-1700. Free. Map 2, C9, p249* Plenty of icky things in formaldehyde, not to mention skeletons and insects.

National Sea Life Centre, Seafront, Bray, **T** 01 286 6939. *Easter-Sep, daily 1000-1700, Oct-Easter, Sat and Sun 1000-1700.* Kids can have close encounters with all kinds of beasties from Irish waters at this marine attraction in Bray. Feeding times and special presentations are open to the public during the summer months.

St Michan's Church, Church St, **T** 01 872 4154, stmichans@iol.ie *Mar-Oct, Mon-Fri 1000-1230 and 1400-1630, Sat 1000-1245, Nov-Feb, Mon-Fri 1230-1530, Sat 1000-1245. €3.50. Map 5, H3, p252* Mummified bodies are the big draw for ghoulish kids.

Activities

Kylemore Indoor Karting, Killeen Rd, Killeen, **T** 01 626 1444, www.kylemore-karting.com *Fri from 1100 (under 18s), Sun from 1000 (9-14s).* Teach your children to be reckless drivers nice and early. Height restrictions apply.

Viking Splash Tours, Bull Alley Street beside St Patrick's Cathedral, **T** 01 855 3000, www.vikingsplashtours.com *Feb-Nov 10 tours per day. €13.50 adults, €7.50 under-13s. Map 2, C4, p248* Put on a silly Viking hat and tour Dublin in a bright, red and yellow amphibious vehicle. The 'Captain' will tell you all about the sites associated with the Vikings before driving straight into the Grand Canal Harbour. Kids will love it.

Kids

Children of Lir
Turned into swans by their stepmother. If the kids won't behave, just tell them this Irish folk tale .

Eating and drinking

Dublin pubs are usually tolerant of children during the day, and most restaurants take the little blighters in their stride too. The streets are littered with every fast-food chain you've ever heard of, plus a few home-grown versions, but there is also a handful of fun spots for more adventurous eaters: try **Thunder Road Café** in Fleet Street, Temple Bar, **T** 01 679 4067, which has video screens and a huge Elvis in the window, or the **Bad Ass Café**, 9-11 Crowne Alley, Temple Bar, **T** 01 671 2596, which has a children's menu and a pulley system to carry your order to the kitchen.

Arts and entertainment

Ark Children's Cultural Centre, 1A Eustace St, Temple Bar, **T** 01 670 7788, www.ark.ie *Opening hours vary.* *Map 3, D5, p250* Programmes in theatre, literature, music and visual arts for children aged four to 14 are supplemented by free entertainment on summer weekends in Meeting House Square. The Ark also runs the **Children's International Theatre Festival**, which runs concurrently with the main theatre festival in October (p177) and features good international and local productions aimed specifically at children. Check the website for details.

Dublin Junior Film Festival, Irish Film Centre, Eustace St, Temple Bar, **T** 01 671 4095. *Map 3, D5, p250*   Usually held between November and December, the festival includes films aimed at pre-teens and teenagers, as well as specialist workshops on movie making.

Airline offices
Aer Lingus, 40-41 O'Connell St Upper, **T** 01 886 8888. **British Airways**, 12 Duke Lane, **T** 1800 626 747. **British Midland**, Nulty Building, Merrion Rd, **T** 01 407 3036. **Ryanair**, Head Office, Dublin Airport, **T** 01 609 7800.

Banks and ATMs
There are branches of **AIB** on Grafton Street, St Stephen's Green and Merrion Road, and branches of the **Bank of Ireland** on Baggot Street Lower, Grafton Street and O'Connell Street. ATMs (24-hour cash machines) are situated outside most banks and usually accept credit cards as well as international debit cards, although there's a small charge. Banks are open Mon-Wed and Fri 1000-1600, Thur 1000-1700; they are closed on Sat and Sun. All banks and larger post offices have currency exchange facilities, and there are dedicated bureaux de change at the airport and tourist offices. There is little difference in cost between changing money in a bank and a bureau de change.

Car hire
The following firms all have desks at Dublin Airport: **Access**, **T** 01 844 4848, www.accesscarrentals.com; **Argus**, **T** 01 862 3811 (pre-booked vehicles only), www.argusrentals.com; **Atlas**, **T** 01 844 4859; **Avis**, **T** 01 605 7555, www.avis.com; **Budget**, **T** 01 844 5159, www.budget.com, and **Hertz**, **T** 01 844 5156, www.hertz.com. **Argus** also has an office at Terenure Road, **T** 01 490 6328; **Avis** is at 1 Hanover Street East, **T** 01 605 7555; **Budget** is at 151 Drumcondra Road, **T** 01 837 9611, and **Hertz** is at 149 Leeson St Upper, **T** 01 660 2255. In addition, most firms have a desk at the Dublin Tourism Centre on Suffolk Street.

Credit card hotlines
American Express T 1800 282 728. **Diners** , **T** 1800 409 2041. **Mastercard**, **T** 1800 557 378. **Visa**, **T** 1800 558 002.

Cultural institutions
Trinity College, College Green, **T** 01 608 1000. **University College Dublin**, Belfield, **T** 01 269 3244. **Goethe Institute**, 62 Fitzwilliam Sq, **T** 01 661 1155, www.goethe.de   **Alliance Français**, 1 Kildare St, **T** 01 676 1732, www.alliance-francais.ie

Dentists
Emergency dental treatment, unlike other medical emergencies, is not covered by European health agreements, and a trip to the dentist can cost around €50. Should you require treatment, your hotel or a local pharmacist should be able to recommend a dentist in the vicinity.

Disabled
Disabled access around Dublin improves a little each year. Several bus routes have wheelchair-friendly vehicles, and all new buses have retractable ramps, wider gangways and priority spaces for wheelchairs. Contact **Dublin Bus** (p218) for further information. The **DART** and other rail services are less accessible, but assistance and wheelchair ramps can be provided with advance notice. Guide dogs are allowed on public transport. Most hotels and restaurants can cater for disabled visitors, but wheelchair access to some of the city's older tourist sights may be restricted. Contact the **Irish Wheelchair Association**, Áras Cúchulainn, Blackheath Drive, Clontarf, **T** 01 818 6400, **F** 01 833 3873, www.iwa.ie, for more detailed information.

Doctors
Only Irish Medical Card holders receive free treatment in Ireland, but EU citizens can reclaim any medical fees or prescription charges by carrying form E111. Expect to a pay about €30 for a consultation with a GP and upwards of €20 for a prescribed medicine. Casualty departments also charge a fee. For the nearest doctor's surgery, enquire at a pharmacy or ask at your hotel.

Electricity

Electricity runs on 220-240V, 50Hz AC. Plugs have three square pins (as in the UK). You may come across the occasional round-pin plug in older establishments, but these are increasingly rare. Adapters can be bought at the airport, in electrical shops around town, or from the Dublin Tourism Centre (p30).

Embassies and consulates

For the address and telephone number of other embassies and consulates in Dublin, consult the Golden Pages. **Australian Embassy**, Sixth Floor, Fitzwilliam House, Wilton Terrace, **T** 01 676 1517. **British Embassy**, 31 Merrion Rd, Ballsbridge, **T** 01 205 3700. **Canadian Embassy**, 65-8 St Stephen's Green, **T** 01 478 1988. **New Zealand Consulate General**, 37 Leeson Park, **T** 01 660 4233. **South African Embassy**, Second Floor, Alexandra House, Earlsfort Centre, Earlsfort Terr, **T** 01 661 5553, **United States Embassy**, 42 Elgin Rd, Ballsbridge, **T** 01 668 8777.

Emergency numbers

For police, fire, ambulance, sea rescue or mountain rescue services, dial 999 or 112.

Hospitals

There are 24-hour accident and emergency departments at **Adelaide and Meath Hospital**, Tallaght, **T** 01 414 3500; **Beaumont Hospital**, Beaumont Rd, **T** 01 809 2714, and **Mater Misericordia Hospital**, Eccles St, **T** 01 803 2000.

Internet/email

Most hotels and hostels offer some kind of internet access for guests although this service can be wildly more expensive than visiting an internet café, where rates start at about five cents per minute, depending on the time of day. Luckily, cyber cafés are in plentiful supply all around the city and are usually open daily until at least 2200. Try one of the following: **Central Cybercafé**, 6 Grafton St, **T** 01 677 8298, www.centralcafe.ie **Does Not Compute**, Unit 2, Pudding Row, Essex St West, Temple Bar, **T** 01 670 4464, www.doesnotcompute.ie **Global Internet Café**, 8 Lower O'Connell St, **T** 01 878 0295, www.globalcafe.ie **Planet Cyber**, 13 St Andrew St, **T** 01 670 5183.

Left luggage
Facilities are provided at **Busáras**, Custom House Quay, **T** 01 703 2434; **Connolly Station**, Amiens St, **T** 01 836 6222, and **Dublin Airport**, **T** 01 814 4633.

Libraries
The main city library is the **Central Library**, ILAC Centre, Henry St, **T** 01 873 4333. It is open to all, but a reader's card is required to borrow books.

Lost property
If you lose anything of value, you should immediately notify the police and contact one of the following: **Airport Police Station**, Dublin Airport, **T** 01 814 4481/666 4950; **Bus Éireann**, Busáras, **T** 01 836 6111; **Connolly Station**, **T** 01 703 2362; **Dublin Bus**, CIE, Earl Place, **T** 01 703 1321; **Heuston Station**, St John's Road West, **T** 01 703 2102.

Media
Newspapers *Irish Times* is the nation's serious newspaper. It's very Dublin centred with good arts reviews and entertainment information on Saturday. The other main broadsheet is the *Irish Independent*, which tends to be rather lightweight and occasionally sensationalist in tone. *The Star* is the chief exponent of Irish tabloid journalism. It's similar to a British tabloid, but the girls keep their clothes on. The *Evening Herald* is an evening version of *The Star* and is useful for movie listings, weekend events, special offers and

sales. *The Sunday Independent* is probably the best of the Irish Sunday papers if you're in Dublin, since like so much of the Irish media, it focusses squarely on news and events in the capital. Among the Sunday tabloids, the *Sunday World* has good coverage of the week's TV as well as oodles of gossip. Most British newspapers are also available in Dublin, although *Sun* readers may be surprised to find that their rag is tidied up a little for the Irish market.

Magazines   Glossy *InDublin* magazine is available fortnightly from newsagents for €2.50 and covers movies, music, gay news, food, books, theatre and visual arts in the city, but the best source of information and commentary is easily the *Event Guide*, a free weekly tabloid newspaper full of useful listings, reviews and interviews. The *Slate* appears monthly, and spares no one's feelings in its reviews of current clubs, bars, restaurants and what's on. Pick it up in shop or pub doorways.

TV   Most Dubliners have some form of cable or satellite service providing Sky and British terrestrial channels. In addition there are four domestic Irish channels. **RTÉ 1** and **RTÉ 2** are pretty interchangeable, with some good local news, excellent history programmes, American movies and soaps, plus one or two locally-made series. **Channel 3** is a Sky One clone that broadcasts lots of US sitcoms and soaps, while **TG4** is the Irish-language programme, full of fiddly-diddly music that really doesn't translate to TV very well, dubbed cartoons and a Gaelic travel programme that can be very entertaining. It also shows some good old American and British movies in the afternoons.

Pharmacies
O'Connell's Late Night Pharmacy, O'Connell St, **T** 01 873 0427. *Mon-Sat 0830-2200, Sun 1000-2200*.

Police

In case of emergency, call 999 or 112. City centre police stations are located at Store Street, **T** 01 855 7761; Pearse St, **T** 01 677 8141; Fitzgibbon St, **T** 01 836 3113; and Harcourt St, **T** 01 475 5555.

Post offices

General Post Office, O'Connell St, **T** 01 705 7000. *Mon-Sat 0800-2000, Sun and bank holidays 1000-1830.* Another useful branch is located on Andrew Street. Open Mon-Fri 0900-1730, Sat 0900-1300. There are sub post offices at Parnell Street, Aston Place, Earlsfort Terrace, Merrion Row, Parkgate Street, Usher's Quay, Ormond Quay Upper and in many other locations around the city centre. Stamps for postage within Ireland and the UK cost 41 cents.

Public holidays

On these days shops, restaurants, pubs and museums may operate Sunday hours or be closed. **New Year's Day** (1 Jan). **St Patrick's Day** (17 Mar, unless it falls on a weekend, in which case the following Mon becomes the public holiday). **Good Friday** (this is not an official holiday, but many businesses treat it as such and pubs are closed all day). **Easter Monday** (Mon following Easter Sunday). **May holiday** (1st Mon in May). **June holiday** (1st Mon in Jun). **August holiday** (1st Mon in Aug). **Autumn holiday** (Mon closest to Hallowe'en). **Christmas Day** (25 Dec, pubs closed all day). **St Stephen's Day** (26 Dec).

Student organizations

USIT (Union of Students in Ireland Travel), 19-21 Aston Quay, **T** 01 679 8833. *Mon-Wed and Fri 0930-1800, Thu 0930-2000, Sat 0930-1700.* USIT can supply an international student identity card to anyone with valid student ID. This card is essential if you intend to claim discounts on transport, admission to sights, ticket prices etc around the city.

Taxi firms

Access Cabs, 20 Baggot St Upper, **T** 01 668 3333. **AtoB**, 40 James St, **T** 01 677 2222. **AAA** 29 Kilbarrack Rd, **T** 01 847 3311. **Alpha 1**, Chamber St, **T** 01 454 1885. **Blue Cabs**, 41 Westland Row, **T** 01 667 7233. **Camden Cabs**, 8 Camden St, **T** 01 475 4000. For further information, see p27.

Telephone

Dublin numbers have seven digits plus an area code (01), which must be dialled if you are calling from outside the city. When phoning Dublin from abroad, dial the international access code, followed by 353 for Ireland, and remember to drop the initial 0 from the Dublin area code.

In Dublin you must always dial the appropriate area code in order to reach a number outside the Dublin area. To phone abroad, dial 00, followed by the international country code (Australia 61; Canada 1; New Zealand 64; South Africa 27; United Kingdom 44; United States 1), the area code (remembering to lose the initial 0), then the number. To phone Northern Ireland, dial 048, then the appropriate area code, then the number. For the operator, dial 100; for directory enquiries, dial 11811.

Public telephones take coins and cards (a sign above the booth indicates your options), and charge about 40 cents for a local call. Readily available pre-paid phone cards offer cheap-rate calls via a code printed on the back. Making phone calls from your hotel room can be very pricey, so always check the rates before you make a call.

Although UK handsets work in Ireland, using your mobile phone in Dublin may also be expensive, particularly if you are charged for receiving calls and text messages. To hire a mobile phone with a local service provider, visit **FoneRental**, 38-40 South Great George's St, **T** 01 671 1401, www.fonerental.com

Time

Dublin (and the rest of Ireland) follows Greenwich Mean Time from the end of October until the end of March, when the clocks go forward one hour to coincide with British Summer Time. The changeovers in each case are well publicized and usually take place on a Saturday at midnight.

Tipping

Tipping is generally practised in restaurants, hairdressers, on long cab journeys and in some toilets, but is entirely at the discretion of the customer.

A standard tip in a restaurant is about 10% of the total bill, although some establishments automatically add on a service charge so that an additional tip is not necessary. Other venues may leave a blank space on your credit card slip to allow you to add a tip to the total amount, although you should not feel constrained to do so. Instead, you may prefer to hand a cash tip to the person who served you.

Toilets

There are good public toilets in the major museums, tourist attractions and in shopping centres, although the latter (such as the St Stephen's Green Centre) may charge for the privilege of using their facilities, and standards of cleanliness can vary depending on the time of day. Department stores also usually have pleasant, though well hidden, toilets. Most pubs have signs indicating that their toilet facilities are for customers only, but it is still often possible to use them discreetly without any trouble. In general, you should avoid public toilets on the street unless they have an attendant.

Note that some toilet signs use the Gaelic words 'Mnà' (women) and 'Fir' (men) rather than the English 'Ladies' and 'Gents'.

Transport enquiries

Dublin Airport, **T** 01 814 4222, for flight information. **Dublin Bus**, 59 O'Connell St Upper, **T** 01 873 4222, www.dublinbus.ie produces a very useful bus map for the city and environs. **Bus Éireann**, **T** 01 836 6111, www.buseireann.ie provides information on national coach services. **Iarnród Éireann**, **T** 01 836 6222, www.irishrail.ie handles enquiries relating to national, suburban and DART rail services.

Travel agents

Thomas Cook, 118 Grafton St, **T** 01 670 9153. **Maxwell's Travel Ltd**, **T** 01 679 5700. **GLA Travel Ltd**, 64 Abbey St, **T** 01 873 1444. **Abbey Travel**, 1 Middle Abbey St, **T** 01 804 7100.

A sprint through history

4000 BC	Early stone age people begIn to practise settled farming in the area around what is now Dublin.
2500 BC	Newgrange passage tomb is built north of Dublin.
300-100 BC	Large areas of Ireland colonized by Iron Age Celts.
AD 200	Dublin is part of Leinster, one of five provinces in Ireland ruled over by Gaelic chieftains.
AD 300-500	Advent of Christianity in Ireland.
AD 5th century	St Patrick's ministry in Ireland. According to legend he establishes a church on the site of present-day St Patrick's Cathedral.
AD 6th-8th century	The Dark Ages. Irish missionaries travel throughout Europe teaching Christianity.
AD 900	Two Celtic settlements exist on the southern banks of the Liffey estuary: Áth Cliath (the ford of the hurdles), at current day Christchurch/Fishamble Street, and Dubh linn (the Black Pool) on the banks of the Poddle, where Dublin Castle now stands.
AD 841-902	Vikings form a pirate settlement at Kilmainham, but are eventually driven out of Ireland by native forces.
AD 917	Vikings successfully establish a base at Áth Cliath and make raids on other settlements in Ireland, trading slaves and captured goods. Dubh linn merges with Áth Cliath and the name is corrupted to form the Viking city of Dyfflin.
936-1022	Constant warfare between native kings and Viking settlers. The Vikings increasingly trade and intermarry with the Irish.

997	Coins are minted and used in Dublin.
1000	Christian churches have been established around Áth Cliath. The citizens of Dyfflin build a *thingmote* (talking place), where College Green now stands.
1014	The Battle of Clontarf takes place north of the Liffey, between Brian Ború, the King of Munster, and the King of Leinster in league with Viking forces. The Vikings are defeated, but Ború is killed and Dublin achieves a degree of autonomy.
1038	Christchurch Cathedral is founded.
1100	Dublin extends westwards.
from 1169	Encouraged by Henry II of England, Norman armies led by the Earl of Pembroke (aka Strongbow) invade Ireland. Henry II's forces take Dublin, which submits to his authority. English power extends beyond Dublin to cover an area known as the 'Pale'.
1192	A stone church is built on the site of present-day St Patrick's Cathedral.
1204	Dublin Castle is built into the city walls at the junction of the Liffey and Poddle rivers.
13th century	Dublin expands as a port, with a population of about 5,000. There are numerous outbreaks of plague and famine. Norman families intermarry with the Gaelic clans to form a largely Gaelic-speaking ruling class.
the 14th century	Dublin's Vikings have become completely assimilated into the Anglo-Gaelic society.

1536-40	Following the break with Rome, Henry VIII dissolves English and Irish monasteries and confiscates church property.
1541	Henry VIII is declared king of Ireland.
1591	The dissolved monastery of All Saints is converted into Trinity College.
1607	The Flight of the Earls leaves large areas of Ulster open for plantation by Protestant settlers. Dublin becomes a military town, with power in the hands of a Protestant minority.
1680-1800	Dublin expands to become the second city in the British Empire, with grand stone buildings and a growing population. Georgian streets and squares are laid out to form the basis of the modern city; the Royal Hospital, Custom House, Four Courts, Leinster House and Mansion House are constructed.
1690	The defeat of Catholic forces by William of Orange at the Battle of the Boyne. Penal Laws are introduced to prevent Irish Catholics from practising their religion, voting or owning land.
1798	Insurrection by the United Irishmen in Counties Dublin, Waterford and Wexford and other parts of the country are suppressed by government forces.
1801	The Act of Union dissolves the Irish Parliament in Dublin. The city experiences a period of economic and social decline, and political unrest grows.
1803	Robert Emmet leads a spectacularly unsuccessful nationalist coup in Dublin.

1828-29	A campaign for Catholic emancipation begun by Daniel O'Connell results in his successful election to the British Parliament, despite the fact that he is forbidden by law to take his seat. As a consequence, the last of the Catholic Penal Laws is repealed.
1841	O'Connell becomes the first Catholic Lord Mayor of Dublin since the time of James II.
1845-49	A series of failed potato harvests brings about the deaths of a million people through starvation and disease. Dublin's population is swelled by desperate people from the countryside coming to the city in search of food. During the following years millions more emigrate. The population of Ireland falls from eight million in 1845 to just 4.5 million in 1901.
1867	Another failed nationalist coup, this time led by the Irish Republican Brotherhood.
1870-82	The Irish Land League, led by Charles Stewart Parnell, campaigns for the right of tenant farmers to buy their land. A series of laws is passed in the British Parliament, instituting land reform and providing the impetus for a move towards Irish Home Rule.
1882	Two English government representatives are murdered by nationalist extremists in Phoenix Park. The event causes political uproar, damaging both Parnell's political career and the cause of Irish Home Rule.
1893	Second Home Rule for Ireland bill is defeated in the British House of Lords.

1913   Terrible work and housing conditions in Dublin
lead to a public strike, known as the Great Lockout.
James Larkin and James Connolly form the Citizen's
Army to protect the strikers, but the uprising is
brutally suppressed by British troops.

A third Home Rule bill comes before Parliament,
but is bitterly opposed by northern Irish Unionists.

1916   Easter Rising. For five days Irish nationalists occupy
strategic positions around the city and declare an
Irish Republic. In the course of the ensuing fighting
almost 500 people die. Fifteen of the rebels are later
executed and many more imprisoned. Although the
uprising fails, it galvanizes support for the cause of
Irish independence.

1918   British elections are held at the end of World War I.
Most Irish seats are won by a new nationalist party
called Sinn Féin, led by Eamon de Valera.

1919-21   The Anglo-Irish War is characterized by guerrilla
warfare on the part of Irish insurrectionists, led by
Michael Collins and Eamon de Valera, and reprisals
by British troops known as the Black and Tans.
In one attack in 1920, Collins' guerrilla forces
assassinate ten British government intelligence
officers in Dublin; in retaliation, the Black and Tans
murder 14 Gaelic football fans at Croke Park.

1920   The province of Northern Ireland is created and
given its own Parliament.

1921   Anglo-Irish Treaty creates the Irish Free State, giving
dominion status to 26 counties of Ireland.

1921-23	Civil War breaks out in Ireland between Collins' party (later Fine Gael), which supports the treaty, and de Valera's party (later Fianna Fáil), which refuses to swear allegiance to the British crown. Street fighting in Dublin.
1932-48	Fianna Fáil wins the general election, putting Eamon de Valera in power. The Irish constitution is written and lays claim to the six counties of Northern Ireland. A censorship law keeps many 20th-century literary classics out of the country. All means of artificial contraception are made illegal. Britain imposes high tariffs on Irish imports, severely damaging Ireland's economy. Dublin suffers from housing and social problems, and a high mortality rate to due to infectious diseases.
1948	New elections bring a coalition government to power, determined to enact social reform. Housing estates are built on the edge of Dublin.
1949	Ireland is finally declared a Republic.
1966	Ireland gradually emerges from economic and social isolation. Dublin celebrates the 50th anniversary of the Easter Rising. Nelson's Pillar on O'Connell Street is blown up.
1969	The first family planning clinic in Ireland is set up in Dublin, but is forbidden by law to supply any contraceptives.
1970-90	Dublin experiences the full force of recession and the negative, knock-on effect of the troubles in Northern Ireland. Thousands of young people leave

the city for Britain or the United States every year in order to find work.

1972	Following the Bloody Sunday murders in Derry, the British Embassy in Merrion Square is burned down.
1990	Mary Robinson becomes first female president of Ireland.
1990s	Celtic Tiger phenomenon. A combination of tax incentives for foreign investors, EU funding and a highly educated workforce leads to an unprecedented economic boom in Ireland. Dublin becomes a vibrant, fast-changing city, characterized by huge building projects, an enormous rise in tourism, and immigration from abroad for the first time since the Normans. House prices in Dublin spiral; drug abuse and associated crime increases.
1993	A condom-vending machine is placed in the toilets of Virgin Records, Eden Quay. Uproar ensues.
1996	Journalist Veronica Guerin is murdered while investigating drug-related crime in Dublin.
1997	A tribunal based in Dublin reveals that the former Taoiseach Charles Haughey had been involved in money laundering in the Cayman Islands.
2000-03	Like other European cities, Dublin is faced with growing numbers of economic immigrants.
2002	Ireland adopts the euro. A downturn in the Irish economy leads to cutbacks in public spending.

Art and architecture

2500 BC Newgrange passage tomb is built using corbelling techniques and complex decorations, including double and triple spirals, and lozenge patterns.

Bronze Age Metal crafts flourish in Ireland in the form of gold torcs, collars and pins, and decorated bronze shields. Settlements consist of simple stone boundaries around hilltop forts.

AD 300-500 Christian monasteries around Ireland produce illuminated manuscripts, such as the Book of Kells, and religious artefacts, such as the Ardagh Chalice.

700-1000 Ireland's first towns consist of simple wooden and wattle huts, enclosed by walls.

1000-1200 Stone buildings are Romanesque in design, with solid walls, arched doorways and simple windows as represented by St Audoen's Church near Christchurch, built in 1190.

1169 The Norman invasion brings continental architecture to Ireland. Larger, Gothic-style stone churches, including Christchurch (1172) and St Patrick's (1192) are built, with ornate triple-arched windows and stained glass. City walls are reinforced with stone. Beyond the city, houses are fortified with curtain walls and towers. Later, Gothic architecture is further refined by the introduction of pointed arches and delicate, ornate windows.

17th century Architecture is no longer motivated by the need for defence, as indicated by the construction of the Royal Hospital at Kilmainham in 1680, one of Dublin's first non-military public buildings.

1680-1800	Much of Dublin's distinctive Georgian architecture is put in place during this period. In its early stages the style is modelled on the neo-classical designs of the 16th-century Italian architect Palladio. Emphasis is laid on symmetry and proportion rather than decoration and ornamentation. The enormous creativity of the time is expressed in the paintings of Nathaniel Hone and George Barrett, and in the plasterwork and wood carvings of Michael Stapleton and the Francini brothers.
1730s	Luke Gardiner begins the development of Georgian north Dublin.
1745	The construction of Leinster House by Richard Castle leads to the development of a new upper-class district south of the river.
1780-1800	James Gandon is the city's pre-eminent architect, designing both the Four Courts (1786) and the Custom House (1791).
19th century	Following the Act of Union, Dublin declines economically and the great building spree of the Georgian period comes to an end. In the arts, portrait painting becomes popular and sentimental; allegorical and biblical paintings by the likes of Francis Danby dominate. Many of Dublin's Catholic churches and the Pro Cathedral are built in the years following Catholic emancipation. In addition, this period sees the construction of public buildings such as the GPO, the railway stations, the museums, prisons and courthouses. The style is eclectic, taking

ideas from the Norman Gothic (as in the renovation of Christchurch) as well as other sources.

1890s Small, red-brick terraced houses are constructed in a grid pattern of streets in Dublin's suburbs. A brief arts and crafts-influenced Celtic revival takes place.

20th century John Lavery and William Orpen are commissioned as official artists during World War I. Later, the paintings of Jack B Yeats and Paul Henry achieve popularity and acclaim. In architecture, modernism, with its stark bare walls, concrete surfaces and plate glass, dominates public design in the city. Major buildings include Busáras by Michael Scott (1940s), the Berkeley Library at Trinity College by Paul Koralec (1967) and the controversial Civic Offices on Wood Quay by Sam Stephenson (1986).

1990-2003 A renewed interest in conservation sees the restoration of the city's Georgian architecture and the regeneration of old buildings to provide for 20th-century requirements. The development of Temple Bar results in a strange mishmash of innovative architecture, kitsch shopfronts and cute street furniture grafted onto the basic pattern of medieval streets. Recent architectural projects include the continued expansion of the green-glass IFSC, the development of the Grand Canal Basin and the construction of the highly acclaimed Ussher Library Building at Trinity College.

Books

Literature has always flourished in Dublin. In the 18th century Jonathan Swift used his writing to upbraid the English government for its mismanagement of his home, and in the 19th century Dublin-born Oscar Wilde dazzled London with his witty repartee and popular plays. William Butler Yeats helped found the Abbey Theatre at the turn of the 20th century, and James Joyce transformed the English novel and encapsulated the Dublin consciousness in *Ulysses* (p232). In fact, the list of great Dublin writers sounds like the reading requirements for a university Eng Lit course, with 20th-century names including Samuel Beckett, Brendan Behan, Sean O'Casey and Flan O'Brien. In modern Dublin, a whole slew of writers have found their voice in the last decade and are telling Dublin's story in drama, prose and poetry. Christy Brown, Hugh Leonard, Sebastian Barry, Roddy Doyle, Joe O'Connor, John Trolan and Emma Donoghue (among many others) have all achieved popular and critical acclaim in recent years.

Fiction

Joyce, J, *Ulysses* (1922), Vintage. The first chapters put most would-be readers off ever finishing the novel. Persevere. Get hold of a recorded reading and listen to the voices of Dublin astonishingly recreated in written form. See also p232.

Ní Dhuibne, É, *The Dancers Dancing* (1999), Blackstaff Press. Young Dubliners attend a summer school in County Donegal in this exploration of sex, politics and Irishness.

O'Connor, J, *Star of the Sea* (2002), Secker and Warburgh. The story of a group of emigrants from Queenstown, County Cork, bound for the United States in 1847.

O'Neill, J, *At Swim, Two Boys* (2002), Scribner. A love story and a political story set in Dublin that breaks new ground in Irish literature. Absolutely wonderful.

Tóibin, B, *The Rising* (2001), New Island Books. A terrific first novel that is both a love story and a dramatization of events leading up to the 1916 Easter Rising.

Non-fiction

Brennan, H, *The Story of Irish Dance* (1999), Brandon. From medieval times to *Riverdance* (of which Ms Brennan heartily approves). A useful study.

Eagleton, T, *The Truth about the Irish* (1999), New Island Books. A laugh a minute, literally, in this alphabet of Irish mores. Worth reading for the entry on B&Bs alone.

Johnson, M, *The Irish Heritage Cookbook* (1998), Wolfhound Press. Surprise your guests with black pudding and bacon salad, boxty, Irish stew, Irish whiskey cake and lots more.

Hamilton, H, *The Speckled People* (2003), Fourth Estate. A beautiful memoir of a 1960s Dublin childhood with a German mother and an Irish father. Makes *Angela's Ashes* seem like sentimental nostalgia.

Harris, N, *Dublin's Little Jerusalem* (2002), A&A Farmar. A history of the area of Dublin around Clanbrassil Street and its inhabitants.

Levy, P, *Culture Shock! Ireland* (2000), Times Editions. Full of insights into the lifestyle and mentality of contemporary Ireland.

Malone, A, *Historic Pubs of Dublin* (2001), New Island Books. The history of some of Dublin's oldest and best-loved watering holes.

Nicholson, R, *The Ulysses Guide: Tours through Joyce's Dublin* (2002), New Island Books. The best practical *Ulysses* guide; it follows the book's 18 episodes through their locations, accompanied by clear maps, directions and summaries.

O'Farrell, M, *A Walk Through Rebel Dublin 1916* (1999), Mercier Press. Well-illustrated guide to the events of Easter 1916. Each chapter takes a different location and gives an account of the blow-by-blow action.

Vallely, F, *Companion to Irish Traditional Music* (1998), Cork University Press. Accompanied by a CD, this is a good reference for the enthusiast.

Ward, M, ed, *In Their Own Voice: Women and Irish Nationalism* (1995), Attic Press. An anthology of women's accounts of the struggle for Irish independence.

Waters, J, *An Intelligent Person's Guide to Modern Ireland* (2001), Bloomsbury. A book that goes against the grain by questioning the worth of Ireland's leap into modernity.

Ulysses

In 1922 Dublin became a major character in what is generally agreed to be the greatest 20th-century novel in the English language, James Joyce's *Ulysses*. Set on 16th June 1904, the day on which James Joyce first walked out with Nora Barnacle (the woman with whom he shared the rest of his life), the novel traces the journey around the city of Leopold Bloom, an Irish Jew. Bloom's wanderings mirror those of the Greek hero Odysseus as he travels home from Troy to Ithaca, and just as the *Odyssey* begins with the story of Odysseus' son, Telemachus, so *Ulysses* opens with the story of Bloom's metaphorical son, Stephen Dedalus.

From his self-imposed exile in Europe, Joyce was assiduous in his efforts to ensure that Bloom's journey around Dublin was technically correct. He took the task very seriously indeed, consulting timetables and getting relatives and friends in Dublin to time journeys, check the location of entrances and so on. Although many of the shops, pubs and other buildings Joyce mentions in the novel have since disappeared, several still stand, and the road layout remains more or less the same as it was in 1904, so it is easy to trace Bloom's movements around the city. Thousands of people enjoy doing this on Bloomsday (p176), which is held annually on the 16th June.

Bloom's home at **7 Eccles Street** in north Dublin is now part of the Mater Hospital, but a plaque marks the spot. The front door of the building was preserved when the house was demolished and is now in the **James Joyce Centre**. After a breakfast of kidneys, Bloom leaves Eccles Street and walks into town along **Gardiner Street**, passing under the railway bridge and crossing **Butt Bridge** to reach the south side of the city. He walks to Westland Row where he notices **Nichol's Undertakers**, still in business nearly a century later. He notes the sleepy congregation in **St Andrew's Church** and continues to the end of Westland Row, passing **Conway's Pub**, now under new management, before stopping at **Sweny's Chemist** (still in business) to buy a bar of soap. As Bloom comments: 'Chemists rarely move.'

Later in the day Bloom walks along **Grafton Street** after watching a Guinness barge go under O'Connell Bridge. At **College Green** he amuses himself over the fact that the statue of Thomas Moore, whose most famous poem is entitled *The Meeting of the Waters*, stands directly over the public toilets.

In Grafton Street Bloom admires the cheerful awnings of the shops, including **Brown Thomas**, which has since moved to the other side of the road, and then goes into **Davy Byrne's**, 'the moral pub', for a gorgonzola sandwich and a glass of burgundy. After lunch he visits the **National Museum**, admires the statues in the foyer and then crosses into the **National Library**. Then he wanders into **Temple Bar** to browse for a second-hand book.

In the late afternoon Bloom passes the **Clarence Hotel** (still there) en route to Ormond Quay, where he stops off at the **Ormond Hotel** (also still in business). From here he wanders into deepest north Dublin and his journey is less easily traced, with fewer businesses still in existence. Dedicated Bloom fans, however, can follow his path well into the early hours of the morning, or even take a trip out to **Howth Head**, remembered with warm sensual affection by Bloom's wife, Molly.

Language

It's been a long time since Gaelic dominated the street sounds of Dublin; you're more likely to hear French or German or Somali being spoken in the city nowadays than Irish. But the language still survives in the capital, even if it isn't used on a daily basis: children learn Gaelic in school; Irish words are used on street signs; and the TV station TG4 broadcasts only in Gaelic (p214).

Dubliners may not flaunt their native language, but they have certainly made English their own. In the market stalls of Moore Street you'll hear the strong vowels of north Dublin: 'book' becomes 'buke', 'queer' rhymes with 'square', people eat a 'sambo' for their lunch and the word 'feck' (apparently evolved from a Gaelic word meaning 'throw') serves as a punctuation mark. Plummier, but just as distinctive, is the accent of Ballsbridge in the south of the city – closer to English received pronunciation, but Irish all the same. It's not just the accent or the vocabulary, though, that distinguishes Dublin English. It's the way that language is used. Dubliners turn their conversations into stories, making up new urban myths on a daily basis, and savouring the sounds of words as much as their meaning. Stop and listen in a pub or on the bus, and you'll be treated to an aural feast.

Glossary

An Óige	(ann oygah) Irish Youth Hostel Association; literally 'the youth'
Bodhrán	(boor-un) hand-held goatskin drum
Craic	(crack) a good time
Dia duit	(jeea dich) hello
Dúchas	(doo-cass) Government department responsible for historic buildings
Fir	(fear) man; used to indicate a gents toilet
Garda	police
Go raibh maith agat	(gurra moih ugut) thank you
Le do thoil	(le du huyl) please
Mná	(mnah) woman; used to indicate a ladies toilet
Slán agat	(slawn ugut) goodbye; to someone who is staying
Slán leat	(slawn lyat) goodbye; to someone who is leaving
Sláinte	(slauntcha) cheers
Taioseach	(tee shookh) Irish Prime Minister
Tanaiste	(tornishta) Irish Deputy Prime Minister
Teach Dail	(teech doyle) Irish MP

Index

A

Abbey Theatre 170
accommodation 103
  gay and lesbian 200
Act of Union 222
adventure sports 193
air travel 21
  airline offices 210
  airlines 22
  Dublin International
    Airport 22
  flight information 218
Anglo-Irish Treaty 224
Anglo-Irish War 224
antique shops 181
Áras an Uachtaráin 80, 81
architecture 227
  Georgian 70, 228
Ardgillan Demesne 100
art 34, 38, 54, 69, **227**
Ashtown Castle 80
Áth Cliath 220, 221
ATMs 210
Aungier Street 45

B

Bacon, Francis 70
Ballsbridge 58
Bank of Ireland 36
Bank of Ireland Arts
  Centre 36, 169
banks 210
bars 147
  gay and lesbian 200
  serving food 125
Beckett, Samuel 33, 66
Behan, Brendan 82
Black and Tans 84, 224
Blackrock 91, 189
Bloody Sunday 226
Bloomsday 71, **176**

Boardwalk 72
Book of Kells **35**, 227
Book of Kells
  Exhibition 34
book shops 183
books 230
Booterstown 91
Ború, Brian 55, 221
Boyne, Battle of the 36, 222
Bray 95
  sights 95
  sleeping 120
Bronze Age 37, **227**
Brú na Bóinne Visitor
  Centre 101
buses 25
  night services 26
  tours 28
Byrne, Gay 39

C

cafés 125
Camden Street 45
car hire 210
Casino at Marino 84
Castle, Richard 37, 44,
  68, 228
castles
  Dalkey 94
  Dublin 50
  Howth 98
  Malahide 99
  Rathfarnham 88
cathedrals
  Christchurch 52
  Pro (Catholic) 67
  St Patrick's 56
Catholic University of
  Ireland 44
Celtic Tiger 9, 16, 33, **226**
cemeteries 55, 82

chancing your arm 57
Chester Beatty Library 51
children 203
Children of Lir 69
Chimney Viewing Tower
  78, 205
Christchurch Cathedral
  52, 221, 227
churches
  Catholic University 44
  St Audeon's 58
  St Michan's 80
  St Stephen's 167
  Whitefriar Street
    Carmelite 46
cinema 161
City Hall 51
city walls 58
Civil War 225
Clarke, Harry 70
Clontarf 82
  Battle of 55, 221
clothes shops 186
clubs 147
  gay and lesbian 200
coach travel 24
coat of arms 52
College Green 33
Collins Barracks 77
Collins, Michael 82, 224
comedy 163
Connolly, James 50,
  56, 224
consulates 212
craft shops 184
credit cards 210
Croke Park **84**, 224
Cúchulainn 67
cultural institutions 211
Custom House 46, **73**
cycling 26

D

Dalkey 94
  eating 144
  sights 94
Dalkey Castle 94
Dalkey Heritage Centre 94
Dalkey Island 94
dance 164
DART **27**, 91
De Valera, Eamon 45, 56, 82, 224, 225
dentists 211
department stores 185
directory 209
disabled 211
doctors 211
Douglas Hyde Gallery 34
drama 169
drinking 125
driving 23, 26
  car hire 210
Dublinn 220
Dublin Bay 91, 96
Dublin Castle **50**, 221
Dublin City Gallery **69**, 169
Dublin Civic Museum 86
Dublin Experience 34
Dublin Film Festival 161, **175**
Dublin International Airport 22
Dublin Theatre Festival 169, **177**
Dublin Tourism 30
Dublin writers 70, **230**
Dublin Writers' Museum **70**, 171
Dublin Zoo **81**, 205
Dublinia **53**, 205
Dun Laoghaire 92
  eating 144
  sights 92
  sleeping 120
Dyfflin 220

E

Easter Rising 44, 46, 55, 62, 66, 69, **224**
eating 125
  Ballsbridge and south 138
  cheap eats 130
  Dalkey 144
  Dun Laoghaire 144
  From Smithfield to the Phoenix Park 144
  Grafton Street and around 127
  Howth 146
  Irish cuisine 134
  kids 208
  late-night 133
  O'Connell Street and around 140
  Skerries 146
  Temple Bar and around 133
  The Liberties and west 137
  vegetarian 137
electricity 212
email 212
embassies 212
emergency numbers 212
entertainment 159
  kids 208
euro 226
events 173
  gay and lesbian 202
  historical 220
excursions 89
  north of Dublin 95
  south of Dublin 91

F

ferry services 24
festivals 173
  gay and lesbian 202
Fianna Fáil 225
film 161

Dublin locations 162
Fine Gael 225
Fitzwilliam Street 41
food shops 188
Forty Foot 93
Four Courts 77
Francis Bacon Studio 69
Fry Model Railway **99**, 205

G

GAA Museum 84
Gaelic 234
Gaelic Athletic Association 84
Gaelic football 84, 193, **194**
galleries 86, 182
  see also under individual entries
Gallery of Photography 47
Gandon, James 36, 73, 228
Garden of Remembrance 69
Gardiner, Luke 71, 228
Gate Theatre 68, **171**
gay and lesbian 197
General Post Office 62, **66**
Glasnevin 82
Glasnevin Cemetery 82
go-karting **193**, 206
gold 37
golf 194
Government offices 39
GPO 62, **66**
Grafton Street 33
Grand Canal 58
Great Famine 223
Great Lockout 66, 224
Gregory, Lady 170
greyhound racing 195
Guerin, Veronica 226
Guinness Storehouse 54

H

Handel's Messiah 80, 175
Ha'penny Bridge 47
Haughey, Charles 226
Helix 168
Henrietta Street 71
Heraldic Museum 87
history 220
Home Rule 223
Hopkins, Gerard Manley 44, 82
horse racing 178, **195**
hospitals 212
hotels 103
House of Lords 36
Houses of Parliament 36
Howth 96
   eating 146
   sights 96
   sleeping 122
Howth Castle 98
Howth Head 96, 98
Hugh Lane Gallery 69
hurling 84, 193, **194**

I

ice-skating 195
internet 212
Ireland's Eye 96
Irish cuisine 134
Irish Jewish Museum 59
Irish Land League 223
Irish Museum of Modern Art 54
Iveagh Gardens 45

J

Jacob's Biscuit Factory 46
James Joyce Centre 71
James Joyce Museum 93
jewellery shops 187
Joyce Tower 93
Joyce, James 45, 66, 71, 93, 176, 232

K

Kavanagh, Patrick 59
kids 203
Killiney 94
Kilmainham 54
Kilmainham Gaol 55
Kilruddery House and Gardens 95

L

language 234
Larkin, James 66, 224
left luggage 213
Leinster House 37, 228
libraries 213
Liffey Boardwalk 72
literature 230
lost property 213

M

MacAleese, Mary 33
magazines 214
Malahide 99
   sights 99
   sleeping 122
Malahide Castle 99
Malone, Molly 36
map shops 183
markets 189
Markiewicz, Countess 44, 56
Marsh's Library 57
Martello tower 93, 94
media 213
   gay and lesbian 199
Meeting House Square **47**, 176, 189
Merrion Square 41
Monto 67
Monument of Light 66
monuments
   see under statues and monuments
Mountjoy Square 71

museums 86
   see also under individual entries
music 165
   classical and opera 167
   rock, pop and traditional Irish 165
   shops 190

N

National Botanic Gardens 83
National Gallery of Ireland 38
National Maritime Museum 92
National Museum of Archaeology and History 37
National Museum of Decorative Arts and History **77**, 205
National Museum of Natural History **39**, 206
National Photographic Archive 47
National Print Museum 88
National Sea Life Centre 95, **206**
National Transport Museum 98
Nelson's Pillar 63, **66**, 225
Newgrange **101**, 220, 227
Newman House 44
newspapers 213
nightlife 147
   gay and lesbian 200
North Bull Island 85
Northern Ireland 224
Number Twenty-Nine 41

O

O'Brien, Flann 73
O'Casey, Sean 73
O'Connell Street 62

O'Connell, Daniel 62, 82, 223
O'Malley, Grace 99
Old Jameson Distillery 78
Old Library 34
opera 167
Orange, William of 36, 222
orchestras 167

P

parks and gardens 42, 45, 69, 80, 83, 95, 100, 101
parliament 37
Parnell Square 68
Parnell, Charles Stewart 62, 82, 223
passage tomb 101
Pearse Museum 88
Pearse, Padraig (aka Patrick) 45, 56, 88
Penal Laws 67, 222, 223
performing arts 159
pharmacies 214
Phoenix Park 80
  assassinations 45, 81, 223
  visitor centre 80
photography 47
picnic spots 142
Plunkett, Joseph 56
police 215
Portobello 58
post 215
Pro Cathedral **67**, 228
Prospect Cemetery 82
public holidays 215
pubs 147
  serving food 125

R

rail travel 25, 27
Rathfarnham Castle 88
red-light district 67
restaurants 125

RHA Gallagher Gallery 88
Robinson, Mary 226
Rotunda Hospital 68
Royal Canal 82
Royal Exchange 51
Royal Hospital 54, 227
rugby 175, **195**

S

sailing 196
Sandycove 93
Seapoint 91
Shaw Birthplace 59
Shaw, George Bernard 59
Shelbourne Hotel 44
shopping 179
Sinn Féin 224
Skerries 100
  eating 146
  sights 100
  sleeping 122
Skerries Watermills and Windmill 100
sleeping 103
  Ballsbridge and south 111
  Bray 120
  Clontarf 119
  Dun Laoghaire 120
  From Smithfield to the Phoenix Park 118
  Glasnevin 119
  Grafton Street and around 106
  Howth 122
  Malahide 122
  price codes 105
  O'Connell Street and around 114
  Skerries 122
  Temple Bar and around 109
  The Liberties and west 111
Smithfield 76

Smithfield Chimney 78
sports 191
St Audeon's Church **58**, 227
St Audeon's Gate 58
St Michan's Church **80**, 206
St Patrick 56, 220
St Patrick's Cathedral **56**, 220, 221, 227
St Patrick's Day **175**, 202
St Stephen's Church 167
St Stephen's Green 42
statues and monuments 34, 36, **42**, 44, 59, 62, 63, 67, 69, 76, 80, 93
Story of the Capital 51
Strongbow 52, 221
student organisations 215
suburbs
  Ballsbridge 58
  Clontarf 82
  Glasnevin 82
  Kilmainham 54
  Marino 84
Swift, Jonathan 33, 57, 81
swimming 196

T

Talbot Botanic Gardens 100
Tara's Palace **99**, 205
taxis 27, 216
telephone 216
television 214
  Dublin locations 162
Temple Bar **46**, 229
ten-pin bowling 196
The Liberties 53
theatre 169
time 217
tipping 217
toilets 217
Tone, Wolf 55
tourist information 30

Index

239

tours **28**, 206
trains 25, 27
transport enquiries 218
travel 21, 25
  air 21
  bus 25
  car 23, 26
  coach 24
  cycling 26
  disabled visitors 211
  enquiries 218
  sea 24
  taxi 27, 216
  train 25, 27
  walking 28
travel agents 218
  discount 22
Treasures of
  Christchurch 52
Trinity College **33**,
  211, 222

U
Ulysses 68, 73, 93, 94,
  176, 230, **232**
University College
  Dublin 211

V
views 53, 54, 76, 78,
  92, 95
Vikings in Dublin 33, 37,
  50, 52, 220
Village quarter 45

W
walking 28
  tours 29
walks 94, 95, 98
War of Independence 76
Waterways Visitor
  Centre 88
Wexford Street 45
whiskey 78

Whitefriar Street
  Carmelite Church 46
Wilde, Oscar 33, 41
wildlife 80, 81, 85, 91, 96
windsurfing 196
winter solstice 101
Wood Quay 52, 53

Y
Yeats, Jack 69, 229
Yeats, William Butler 170

Z
zoo 81

Best boxes
Cheap eats 130
Cool bars 152
Galleries 50
Georgian architecture 70
Guesthouses 109
Hostels 107
Late-night food joints 133
Mid-range hotels 110
Picnic spots 142
Restaurants for special
  occasions 129
Statues and
  monuments 42
Top-notch hotels 108
Unreconstructed Dublin
  pubs 151
Veggie venues 137
View points 76

Credits

Footprint credits
Text editor: Sophie Blacksell
Series editor: Rachel Fielding

Production: Jo Morgan, Mark Thomas
In-house cartography: Claire Benison,
Kevin Feeney, Robert Lunn,
Sarah Sorensen
Proof-reading: Elizabeth Barrick

Design: Mytton Williams
Maps: Footprint Handbooks Ltd

Photography credits
Front cover: Farrell Grehan/CORBIS
(door at Doheny & Nesbitt)
Inside: Patrick Donald,
www.dublinphotographs.com and
Dublin Tourism, www.visitdublin.com
(p1 statue of Molly Malone, p5 memorial
in Prospect Cemetery, p31 Dublin door
knocker, p89 lighthouse in Dublin Bay)
Generic images: John Matchett
Back cover: Patrick Donald
(Custom House)

Print
Manufactured in Italy by LegoPrint
Pulp from sustainable forests

Publishing information
Footprint Dublin
2nd edition
Text and maps © Footprint Handbooks
Ltd June 2003

ISBN 1 903471 66 4
CIP DATA: a catalogue record for this
book is available from the British Library

® Footprint Handbooks and the Footprint
mark are a registered trademark of
Footprint Handbooks Ltd

Published by Footprint Handbooks
6 Riverside Court
Lower Bristol Road
Bath, BA2 3DZ, UK
T +44 (0)1225 469141
F +44 (0)1225 469461
E discover@footprintbooks.com
W www.footprintbooks.com

Distributed in the USA by
Publishers Group West

Publishing stuff

Complete title list

Latin America & Caribbean

Argentina
Barbados (P)
Bolivia
Brazil
Caribbean Islands
Central America & Mexico
Chile
Colombia
Costa Rica
Cuba
Cusco & the Inca Trail
Dominican Republic
Ecuador & Galápagos
Guatemala
Havana (P)
Mexico
Nicaragua
Peru
Rio de Janeiro
South American
  Handbook
Venezuela

North America

Vancouver (P)
Western Canada

Africa

Cape Town (P)
East Africa
Libya
Marrakech &
  the High Atlas
Morocco
Namibia
South Africa
Tunisia
Uganda

Middle East

Egypt
Israel
Jordan
Syria & Lebanon

Asia

Bali
Bangkok & the Beaches
Cambodia
Goa
India
Indian Himalaya
Indonesia
Laos
Malaysia
Myanmar (Burma)
Nepal
Pakistan
Rajasthan & Gujarat
Singapore
South India
Sri Lanka
Sumatra
Thailand
Tibet
Vietnam

Australasia

Australia
New Zealand
Sydney (P)
West Coast Australia

Europe

Andalucía
Barcelona
Berlin (P)
Bilbao (P)
Bologna (P)
Copenhagen (P)
Croatia
Dublin (P)
Edinburgh (P)
England
Glasgow
Ireland
London
Madrid (P)
Naples (P)
Northern Spain
Paris (P)
Reykjavik (P)
Scotland
Scotland Highlands
  & Islands
Spain
Turkey

(P) denotes pocket
Handbook

For a different view…
choose a Footprint

Over 90 Footprint travel guides
Covering more than 145 of the world's most exciting
countries and cities in Latin America, the Caribbean, Africa, Indian
sub-continent, Australasia, North America, Southeast Asia, the
Middle East and Europe.

Discover so much more…
The finest writers. In-depth knowledge. Entertaining and accessible.
Critical restaurant and hotels reviews. Lively descriptions of all the
attractions. Get away from the crowds.

Footprint feedback

We try as hard as we can to make each Footprint guide as up-to-date and accurate as possible but, of course, things always change. Many people write to us, with corrections, new information, or simply comments. If you'd like to let us know about that quirky bar or restaurant, underground club or locals' hangout that you've uncovered, or that great little place to stay, we'd be delighted to hear from you. Please give us as precise information as possible, quoting the edition number and page number. Your help will be greatly appreciated, especially by other free-spirited travellers. In return we will send you details about our special guidebook offer.

Email Footprint at:

dub2_online@footprintbooks.com

or write to:
Elizabeth Taylor
Footprint Handbooks
6 Riverside Court, Lower Bristol Road
Bath BA2 3DZ UK

246

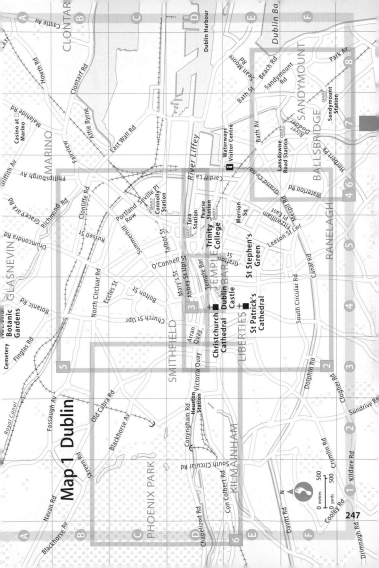

Map 1 Dublin

247

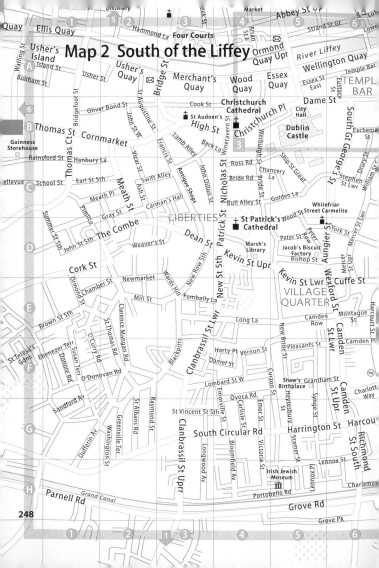

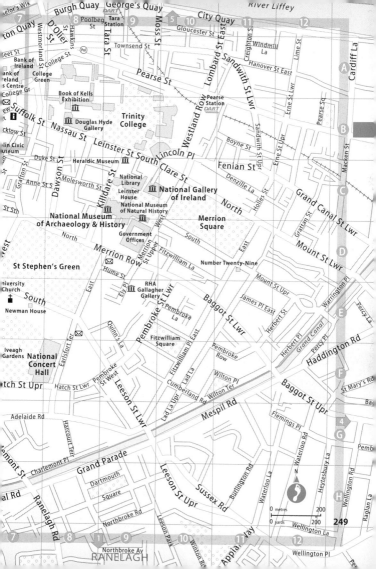

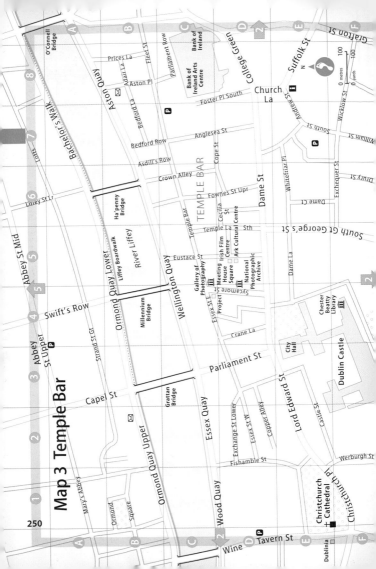

Map 3 Temple Bar

250

A **B** **C** **D** **E** **F**

O'Connell Bridge
Prices La
Fleet St
Adair La
Aston Pl
Parliament Row
Bank of Ireland
Bank of Ireland Arts Centre
College Green
Suffolk St
Grafton St
Church La
Foster Pl South
Andrew St
South St
Wicklow St
William St
Bachelor's Walk
Aston Quay
Bedford La
Bedford Row
Anglesea St
Asdill's Row
Crown Alley
Cope St
TEMPLE BAR
Fownes St Upr
Dame St
Whitefriar Pl
Exchequer St
Drury St
Ha'penny Bridge
Temple Bar
Cecilia St
Temple La Sth
Dame Ct
Dame La
South Gt George's St
Liffey Boardwalk
River Liffey
Ormond Quay Lower
Millennium Bridge
Wellington Quay
Eustace St
Gallery of Photography
Meeting House Square
Irish Film Centre
Ark Cultural Centre
National Photographic Archive
Project
Essex St E
Sycamore St
Crane La
Chester Beatty Library
Liffey St Lr
Abbey St Mid
Abbey St Upper
Swift's Row
Strand St Gt
Capel St
Grattan Bridge
Parliament St
City Hall
Dublin Castle
Lord Edward St
Castle St
Mary's Abbey
Ormond Square
Ormond Quay Upper
Essex Quay
Exchange St Lower
Essex St W
Copper Alley
Fishamble St
Wood Quay
Werburgh St
Christchurch Cathedral
Christchurch Pl
Wine Tavern St
Dublinia

N
0 metres 100
0 yards 100

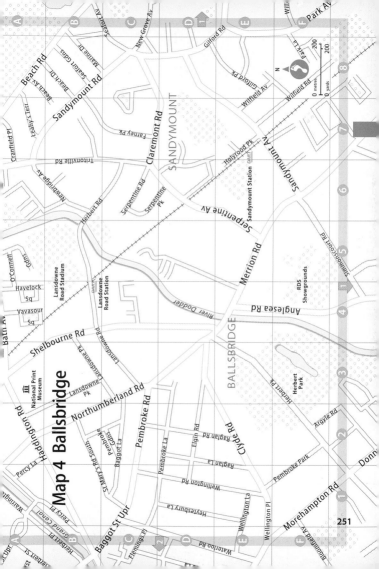

Map 4 Ballsbridge

251

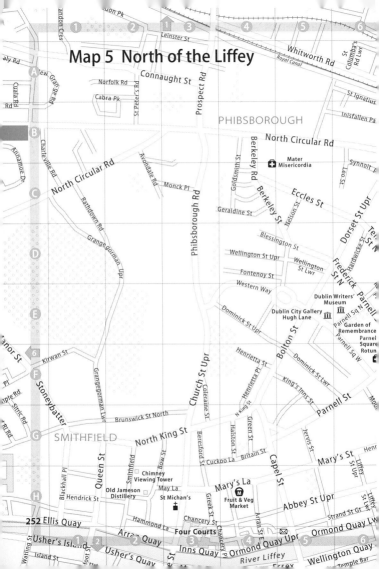

Map 5 North of the Liffey

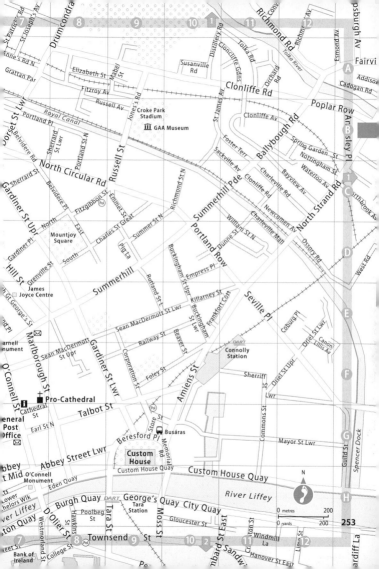

Map 6 Phoenix Park & Kilmainham

Áras an Uachtaráln

PHOENIX PARK

To US Ambassador's Residence

North Rd

Polo Rd

Spa Rd

Dublin Zoo

To Papal C

Acre Rd

Lord's Walk

Zoo Rd

To Cromlech

Kyber Rd

Chesterfield

Magazine Fort

Wellington Rd

Military Rd

Chapelizod Rd

River Liffey

South Circular Rd

N

Irish National War Memorial Park

0 metres 200
0 yards 200

254

KILMAINHAM

Con Colbert Rd

Inchicore Rd

Bully's Acre

Sarsfield Rd

Kilmainham Gaol

Dunsir Av

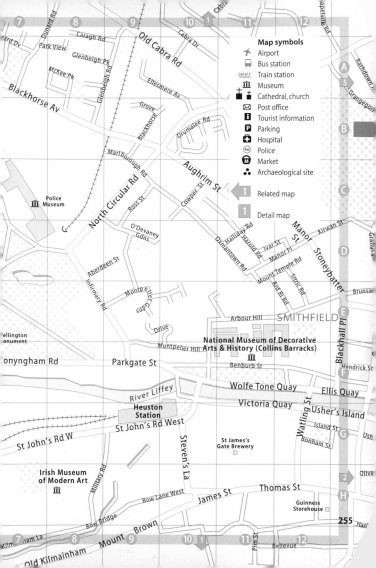

Map symbols

✈ Airport
🚌 Bus station
🚆 Train station
🏛 Museum
✝ Cathedral, church
✉ Post office
ℹ Tourist information
Ⓟ Parking
✚ Hospital
Pol Police
🏪 Market
⁘ Archaeological site
➤**1** Related map
1 Detail map

7 Park View
Stuart Dv
Dunard Rd
Caragh Rd
McKee Pk
Glenbeigh Pk
Glenbeigh Pk
8
Old Cabra Rd
Ellesmere Av
9
Cabra Dr
10
Cabra Dr
1
Cabra
11
Rathdown Rd
Grangegor
Grapeville Rd
12

A
5
Grangegor

Blackhorse Av
Grove
Blackhorse
Drumalee Rd
B

Marlborough Rd
North Circular Rd
Aughrim St
Cowper St
C

🏛 Police Museum
Ross St
O'Devaney Gdns
Halliday Rd
Harold Rd
Oxmantown Rd
Ivar St
Manor Pl
Mount Temple Rd
Manor St
Kirwan St
Stoneybatter
Stirc Rd
Ard Rd Rd
Brunsw
D

Aberdeen St
Infirmary Rd
Montpelier Gardens
Drive
Arbour Hill
Montpelier Hill
SMITHFIELD
Blackhall Pl
E

Wellington Monument
National Museum of Decorative Arts & History (Collins Barracks)
🏛
Benburb St
Hendrick St
F

onyngham Rd
Parkgate St
River Liffey
Wolfe Tone Quay
Ellis Quay
Watling St
Usher's Island

Victoria Quay
Island St
Bonham St
G
🚆 Heuston Station
St John's Rd West

St John's Rd W
St James's Gate Brewery
Olive
2

🏛 Irish Museum of Modern Art
Military Rd
Steven's La
Bow Lane West
James St
Thomas St
Guinness Storehouse
H

Bow Bridge
Mount Brown
Bow Lane West
James St
Prim St
Bellevue
255
Han'

Kilm nham La
7
Old Kilmainham
8
9
10
1
11
12

Map 7 Around Dublin

Irish Sea

Slane
Drogheda
Newgrange
M1
River Boyne
N1
Laytown

Duleek

Kentstown

M E A T H

Balbriggan

Naul

Ardgillan Demesne

Skerries

Garristown

D U B L I N

Lusk

Rush

Dunshaughlin

Ashbourne

N1

Portraine

N3

N2

Donabate

Swords

Malahide

Portmarnock

Dunboyne

Ireland's Eye

M1

Howth

Maynooth

M50

N1

Howth Head

To Holyhead & Liverpool

M4

Phoenix Park

North Bull Island

Celbridge

Lucan

DUBLIN

Dublin Bay

Straffan

Booterstown

Blackrock

Dun Laoghaire

To Holyhead

Sandycove

Dalkey

Dalkey Island

Rathcoole

Killiney

N7

M11

N81

Bray

K I L D A R E

Bray Head

Glencree

Enniskerry

Kilruddery House & Gardens

W I C K L O W

N11